The Uniqueness of Waldorf Education

The Uniqueness
of Waldorf Education

by Astrid Schmitt-Stegmann

Rudolf Steiner College Press

Publication of this book was made possible by a grant from the Waldorf Curriculum Fund.

Cover art: © by Iris Sullivan
Cover design: Claude Julien, Astrid Schmitt-Stegmann, John Wihl

ISBN 978-0-9818095-5-7

The content of this book represents the view of the author and should not be taken as the official opinion or policy of Rudolf Steiner College or Rudolf Steiner College Press.

Book orders may be made through
The Bookstore at Rudolf Steiner College:
Tel. 916-961-8729
Catalog and online orders: www.rscbookstore.com
E-mail: bookstore@steinercollege.edu

Rudolf Steiner College Press
9200 Fair Oaks Boulevard
Fair Oaks, CA 95628, USA

I dedicate this book to Waldorf teachers,
honoring their tireless and committed work
with children every day.

"It may perhaps be clear to you what all education and teaching in the Waldorf School is designed to bring about. It aims to bring up children to be human beings strong and sound in body, free in soul, lucid in spirit. Physical health and strength, freedom of soul, and clarity of spirit are things humankind will require in the future more than anything else, particularly in social life. But in order to educate and teach in this way, it is necessary for the educator to acquire…complete discernment of the child's organism, and it must be a discernment of the organism enabling them to judge physical health…and… bring it into harmony with the soul."

The Spiritual Ground of Education, Rudolf Steiner

Contents

Part I -- Education as a force for healing

Part II -- Practical classroom work: the role of rhythm and pictures in teaching

Part III -- The path of the Waldorf teacher

Foreword

I am exceedingly happy to write a foreword for Astrid Schmitt-Stegmann's book. I have known her for decades as an engaged Waldorf teacher and instructor in various Waldorf teacher education programs. I was part of those individuals around her who always encouraged her to write down her experiences and insights. This book is clear and well-formed, very interesting and stimulating to read. It is an enthusiastic testimonial to a pedagogy that serves head, heart, and hand, a thoroughly artistic education.

Astrid addresses the Waldorf education approach fundamentally in the first part of her book. It becomes clear how this education trusts in the healthy, innate potentials within each human being and intends to develop and strengthen these.

We clearly see this in the "individual verses" in this book. The teacher creates these for each child to foster the individual journey of the child. Waldorf education also communicates the historical development of humankind and its diverse peoples and cultures in such a way that from early on respect, admiration, and sympathy may grow as well as the desire to understand this world in which we live.

The path of a Waldorf teacher gives the possibility for tremendous growth and transformation as indicated in the third part of the book.

As a pediatrician I know how many functional disorders and soul traumas have their cause in an education in which the developing child, his needs and possibilities find too little respect and acceptance. The greater is the gratitude for educators like Astrid, who devote their life to bring change and healing in this respect.

Michaela Gloeckler, MD
Medical Section, Goetheanum, Dornach, Switzerland
14 April 2015

Words of Gratitude

In this second decade of the twenty-first century this publication by Astrid Schmitt-Stegmann arrives at a crucial moment. All people who have worked with children and with colleagues in Waldorf schools or in other situations will recognize immediately when reading this book that significant practical spheres of help are offered to them.

Every part of this book may prove to be essential for education in our time and especially for Waldorf education as the teacher enjoys a greater freedom of working with a curriculum drawn from the deep knowledge of the human being, which Rudolf Steiner could access.

The principles which the author presents in this book in a very clear manner are those which may strengthen every teacher in his or her commitment to working with children and young people. Every aspect of the method of Waldorf Education is indispensably helpful for each child, be it the rhythmic part of the day or a musical experience or a story or the use of color.

Nevertheless, to the degree that the teacher knows the inner reason for a healthy education, a transformative education for the developing human being, the greater the effect will be on the child.

Also as this work demonstrates, the effect is not limited to the child but extends in a wonderful way to the teacher who is the creator in the educational process for each group of children, for each child.

Astrid Schmitt-Stegmann, out of her many years of experience as a Waldorf school teacher and as a foremost educator for teachers, brings the fruits of her experiences also in relationship with colleagues, for no school can be a school without colleagues.

It is with great enthusiasm that I congratulate my colleague in Waldorf education for the accomplishment of this book! I am sure that many educators from many streams of education will welcome this book with deep gratitude, for it provides answers to the most pressing questions which we all can share today in regard to the education of our children and youth.

Virginia Sease, PhD, Emeritus
Executive Council at the Goetheanum, Dornach, Switzerland
15 April 2015

Introduction: Why I wrote this book

Having worked as a Waldorf class teacher and specialty teacher for some seventeen years and then as a teacher of Waldorf teachers for more than twenty years in Europe, North America, and Asia, my heart beats for Waldorf education. I love its uniqueness. Through this education we learn to admire, yes, even be in awe of the work of art each human being is - capable of a whole range of inner soul responses, capable of taking hold of self and the world with an amazingly resourceful, individual spirit. The depths of insight into the human being and human development of Rudolf Steiner, the founder of Waldorf education, is for me a daily source of inspiration and a deeply significant path of discovery.

During the last twenty years of my career as an educator, and as advisor, mentor, and evaluator in Waldorf schools throughout the world and in Waldorf charter schools in the US, I have observed a slow decline in inner strength, will, and commitment of incoming teachers in penetrating the essence of Waldorf education. At the same time, a focus on teaching methods has become ever more prevalent. The richness, depth, and healing power innately present in Waldorf education is being weakened, even lost.

In this book I address particularly Steiner's expectation that every Waldorf teacher should know the effect each subject has on the growth and development of each child. Steiner speaks to the teachers about these effects in his many lectures on education, so also in the collection titled, *Study of Man*. There in the first lecture, he says that as teachers "we must be conscious of what we are doing, right down to the foundations."

With this book, I am speaking to those of you who are Waldorf teachers or wish to become Waldorf teachers. Beyond that, I am writing for everyone seeking a greater understanding of children and how they learn, and of the nature of the human being and of human development. Teachers, home-schoolers, and parents may find these pages rewarding as they reveal the genius that comes to expression in the indications given by Rudolf Steiner. To understand them genuinely calls for an open mind, open heart, and interest.

My hope is that, even if only in a small way, I can waylay the erosion of knowledge concerning the human being and human development and of many of Steiner's other valuable insights. Without an in-depth understanding of the developing child, a teacher's creative ideas and imaginations that truly help the child will be hard to come by.

In addition to an in-depth knowledge of human nature, becoming a Waldorf teacher involves the patient work of self-transformation. This is an essential part of the teacher's work, for as teachers we have a strong impact on the students, not only on the soul and spirit, but right down into physical health and illness.

When we speak of Waldorf education, we must be clear from the beginning that we are entering a distinct and unique educational paradigm. The premise here is that it is impossible for any true educational activity to occur in the classroom without having a detailed, in-depth knowledge of the nature of the human being and of human development. We have to know what it means to be human before we can educate! As Rudolf Steiner said, "All true teaching, all true pedagogy must be based on knowledge of human nature."[1]

*

Every now and then I hear from beginning teachers the sentiment, "Don't tell me all those other things. Just show me what to do in the classroom." This attitude alarms me, as I have seen it lead directly to problems. For one, through lack of individual understanding and insight Waldorf practices may become narrow, limited, and consequently dogmatic. This can occur, for instance, when a teacher has no clear understanding of how she herself as well as her presentation and delivery of each subject affects the child right into the bodily constitution. If the focus is merely on the "what," and to some extent on the "when" but not on the "why," the freedom of each teacher to be individually creative, artistic, imaginative–so crucial to this education–is in jeopardy. Then, a new teacher may follow what she sees another teacher do without understanding where the other teacher's practices originated, why she is doing them, and how they affect the child. A teacher's inner freedom, so important to Rudolf Steiner, depends on penetrating to a level of clarity concerning the what (subject), the how, and the when, and all importantly, the why.

As a class teacher I loved the approach Waldorf education takes with all activities. In the Main Lesson, the whole child is addressed every day; his thinking, feeling, and will are strengthened and nurtured; movement and activity are integrated; the arts are practiced and send their healing impulses into the child while strengthening his will. Each teacher can introduce learning with imagination and creativity and witness how through this approach the students are motivated to engage, to be interested, to love learning. To achieve this is challenging in our present time when children are influenced by so much that hinders them from building up their inner strength to pay attention, focus, learn, and think.

It is truly worthwhile to go over the indications given by Steiner again and again in order to penetrate them and to discover what specifically they address in the child, and also to realize that certain aspects that Steiner gave in his time were not at all as crucial to know then as they are now. Steiner rarely addressed only the needs of his time.

It is fascinating to realize the deeper levels at which his classroom management suggestions aim, so that they stimulate the child's individual "I" to engage itself. (See pedagogical stories and individual verses in Part II of this book). He aims at stimulating and encouraging the child from inside, and he wants to guide will-engagement through moral images in the stories. As educators we need to see clearly that Steiner's goal is to self-activate the child's will. With this, Steiner lays the groundwork for what later in life blossoms into self-motivation and self-responsibility. All activities and impressions of the young child pass down into substrates of existence, and what has been laid in the body of the child at a young age reappears in later life as capacities. This kind of insight is what makes Waldorf education so immensely valuable.

9

In this book, I focus on unique aspects of Waldorf education that differentiate Rudolf Steiner education from other types of approaches. If we only scratch the surface, that is, if we focus merely on methods, we might still have a delightful and broad education and curriculum, but we will not draw from the deeper waters of the well where the purest, healthiest waters are.

*

This book has three parts that address the three major areas of concentration for a Waldorf teacher. However, I make no claim of completeness in the thoughts and materials presented here. Yet, my hope is that they will enable my readers to bring life and health to children from the well-springs.

Part I of this book aims to help teachers and parents broaden and deepen their understanding of the growing child, and indicates how to support these precious, developing human beings in their process of becoming capable, independent, mature adults.

Part II focuses on classroom activities unique to Waldorf education. Teachers who already include some of these activities in their classroom may learn here helpful details and perspectives, while those teachers who do not use them as yet are invited to incorporate them.

Part III focuses on some of the self-transformative work necessary for Waldorf teachers and, for that matter, for every adult individual. Being grounded in a contemplative, meditative practice is necessary for the teacher in order to be a healthy model and a guiding light for the children.

When in Waldorf education we speak of teaching the whole human being, it's sometimes phrased as "teaching head, heart, and hand." This brief response answers the question, "What is Waldorf education?" on some level. We as teachers understand that human beings have far greater, stronger, and subtler capacities than those visible in the physical body.

For me as Waldorf teacher, it was incredibly rewarding to come gradually to a more direct experience of the subtler bodies of the human being. We then begin to perceive children in new and more differentiated ways. We teachers can begin to read subtleties that come to expression in the way the child looks at us, in the way the child sits, walks, gestures (or not!), speaks. All of these take on a personal expression with each child. It is a great joy for the teacher to experience the individuality of the child shine through all of these expressions. Teachers need to sensitize themselves to perceive and understand the working of the subtler bodies, which need to be addressed and nurtured.

Steiner's insights make such expanded understanding possible for us, but only if we are willing to make inner efforts to develop it. In our present time of rapid access to information taking the time to develop such insight may be challenging. However, dear teaching colleagues, there is wisdom in that familiar saying, "No pain, no gain." We need to ask ourselves, "Who are we without idealism, without striving, without aspiring to develop our true Self?"

So, let us begin our journey. It is an exciting one.

Astrid Schmitt-Stegmann
Fair Oaks, CA
May 2015

Acknowledgements

I wish to express my heartfelt thanks to:

Janey Newton Norton for her friendship and support.

MariJo Rogers for her willingness to edit my English that now and then slipped back into the German habit of endlessly long sentences! Her patience and skill are remarkable. She was a great help throughout the process.

Iris Sulllivan whose beautiful artistry is on the cover of the book. She showed amazing flexibility and understanding as my original imagination changed and metamorphosed.

Faith Moore for tooth combing the whole text with great attention – one more time.

Claude Julien of Rudolf Steiner College Press for all of his advice and support to guide the publication of this book through the publishing meanders.

Dr. Michaela Gloeckler, to use excerpts and drawings from her work as needed.

Susan Kerndt, Kathleen Fenton, and Simone Rogers for giving permission to use one of their stories.

My daughter Daniela and her husband Jonathan, who provided photographs of their children to illustrate aspects of child development.

My parents Carl and Christine Stegmann whose love for and dedication to the work of Rudolf Steiner was inspirational for me.

Astrid Schmitt-Stegmann

Part I -- Education as a force for healing

The teacher as healer

One of the impulses of Rudolf Steiner education is its focus on healing. This is possible only by understanding that education affects the *whole* human being. Rudolf Steiner made Waldorf teachers aware again and again that they do not affect and form only the soul-spiritual life of the child but that teaching at all times affects also the physical body, bringing about either health or illness.

In the year 2000, a dissertation written by Theodor Zdrazil, at the University of Bielefeld, Germany, discussed the healing effects of Waldorf education. He wrote, "Waldorf education is the most radical and far-reaching health-supportive education in our time!"[2]

This healing element is embedded in all aspects of Waldorf education. In order for the teacher to access it, she has to be interested in striving for an ever more penetrating understanding of the human being and of human development. For me some of the more exciting moments in my teaching days were when I experienced my insight increase as I got better and better at reading the children, reading their gazes and facial expressions, the expression of their movements and gestures, their walk, the "talk" of their hands, the quick changes in the moods called forth by the teacher's descriptive speech and by the lively images of the story material.

How connected, trusting, impressionable, vulnerable, how open, and ready to be filled with wonder and awe an unspoiled young child is (which is even rarer in our present time). What a gift! Seeing children in this way felt almost miraculous to me. I felt that as teachers we experience at times what can only be called a piece of heaven in the presence of a child.

I noticed early on how conscious the teacher needs to be when guiding these young souls, especially with the diverse challenges that children currently bring with them. And although as teacher we must, of course, know as much as possible about each child, she must avoid becoming too focused on children's challenges, for then she may lose sensitivity and sight of the deeper layers, the as yet hidden qualities of the child. Every child carries the future as seed within, and as parent or teacher or faculty member, we must not get stuck and become fixed on the elements of the past. We should find a way to the will of the child, the artistic-creative element. The will is pure potential, is the future. The will wells up from deeper levels, and it is particularly these deeper layers that we must reach as Waldorf teachers, as it is there where we can reach the forces of health.

In a lecture given in 1920 in Forest Row, England, Rudolf Steiner points out, "We can only educate rightly when education is seen as a healing process," and when the educator is conscious: "I should be a healer."[3] In lectures given by Steiner that same year in Ilkley in northern England, he states, "All education is for the child a bodily education, for all soul-spiritual education works at the same time into the physical body. This is the secret of human development: What lives in soul and spirit at a certain time in life will manifest later on in the body as health and illness."[4]

If, as teacher, we really say to ourselves, "I want to be a healer," then we must first and foremost strive for a comprehensive understanding of these unfolding conditions of the child's physical, psychological, and spiritual capacities.

To come to such an understanding, we draw on Rudolf Steiner's insight that makes it possible for the teachers to become healers. For life is a whole, and what is experienced in the first third of life is reflected in the last third when we experience the effects as living consequence!

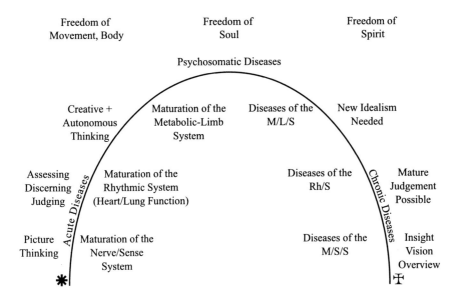

| Freedom of Movement, Body | Freedom of Soul | Freedom of Spirit |

Psychosomatic Diseases

| Creative + Autonomous Thinking | Maturation of the Metabolic-Limb System | Diseases of the M/L/S | New Idealism Needed |

| Assessing Discerning Judging | Maturation of the Rhythmic System (Heart/Lung Function) | Diseases of the Rh/S | Mature Judgement Possible |

Acute Diseases — Chronic Diseases

| Picture Thinking | Maturation of the Nerve/Sense System | Diseases of the M/S/S | Insight Vision Overview |

✳ ☩

Life is a whole.

See also in: Michaela Gloeckler, Education – Health for Life, 2006, Medical Section, Goetheanum, Dornach, Switzerland, 10.

A "must" in Waldorf education

Comprehensive knowledge of the child is a "must" in Waldorf education. One of the fundamental principles of the art of this teaching is to work from the whole to the part. This approach is grounded in a teacher's steady and continuing exploration of human nature–what it means to be human and what it means for a human being to develop. Rudolf Steiner speaks about this subject frequently. Here are three passages from a collection of his lectures on education titled, *The Roots of Education*, that I encourage you to read slowly and thoughtfully and return to as inspiration for your daily work in the classroom.

> A concrete knowledge of the human being is of the utmost importance in human life. A really concrete knowledge of the human being, with the power of seeing right into the human himself, is the only possible basis for a true art of education.[5]

[We must have a] comprehensive knowledge of the human being, a truly penetrating knowledge…it is not enough to have certain rules of how [the child] should be taught and educated, and then just conform to the rules…this will never lead to good teaching. We must bring inner fire, an inner enthusiasm to our work; we must have impulses which are not intellectually transmitted from teacher to child according to certain rules, but which pass over from teacher to child in an intimate way. The whole of our being must work in us as educators, not only the thinking…but also the feeling and…the will must play their part.[6]

[We] see that the human being possesses three clearly distinct members: a physical body, a soul, and a spirit. And we can only see the whole human being if we have the wisdom and knowledge to recognize the soul in its true nature as clearly as we recognize the physical body; and further, if we are able to recognize the spirit…as an independent being.[7]

The subtler bodies

We are used to our physical body. There it is, clearly before us at all times. We look at ourselves. We look at others. We learn anatomy and physiology that enlighten us about the body's organs, organ processes, and structures. Yet we can easily see that human beings are more than physical, material substance. We have shape. We grow and change. Rudolf Steiner calls the forces that accomplish growth and change the life-and-forming forces, or the etheric body. These forces work in close connection with the physical body, shaping and elaborating it and its various organs and organ processes, especially during the first six to seven years of a child's life.

We also know that human beings have thoughts and feelings, an inner life. Steiner speaks here of the soul, also called the astral body, that comprises the inner, personal space of an individual. Finally, we recognize that each person is a unique entity with ideals and aspirations. This Steiner calls the human

"I", the human spirit, the individual's essential and eternal Self, that part of each of us that has gone and will continue to go through many incarnations.[8]

As educators we know, of course, that nothing at all is accomplished by being able just to apply names to these subtler bodies. Naming must be substantiated by our gaining the capacity to see how each of these subtler bodies expresses itself in the child before us, how we as teachers can nourish and strengthen these bodies, or conversely, how we might influence them in a negative way. Each of the subtler bodies has an effect on the physical body, and they also affect each other. The ideal for an educator therefore should be: to work continually on understanding the physical, etheric, and astral bodies of the human being and, in addition, be aware of the effect that I, as teacher, have on these bodies of the child, an effect I have through who I am and through my teaching style. We should also be clear on the effect each subject has on the child.

Yes, that is a tall order! And yes, to strive more and more for insight into the working of these subtler bodies over the years of teaching is not only a necessity but a joy for any serious Waldorf educator. For in our present time and even more so in the future, children will bring greater gifts but also greater challenges into the classroom. Restlessness, uncontrolled movement, inability to listen and focus, constant talking or difficulty getting engaged in what is asked of them–these traits are only the tip of the iceberg of challenges that are a general experience of teachers in the present-day classroom.

By acquiring a sensitive and detailed understanding of the human body, soul, and spirit, a pedagogical instinct awakens in the teacher that develops much-needed healing capacities.

The physical body

Having a picture of the various bodies of the human being, we can turn to the physical body itself. This is the body connected with the physical world. As Steiner says, "This human physical body is subject to the same laws of physical existence and is built up of the same substances and forces as the world as a whole...substances that mix, combine, form, and dissolve through the same laws that also work in the substances within the mineral world."[9]

The physical bodies of the children create pictures for us. We stand on the playground and see the lightness of first graders in their bodies, clearly visible when they are running and seem hardly to touch the ground! The lift of the body and the ease and joy of movement is remarkable. We can compare that to a fourteen- or fifteen-year-old, where an experience of the gravity forces creates a different picture, one of heavy weight that has to be dragged along (except, of course, when there is something they themselves want to do!). To ask eighth graders to stand straight without leaning against something seems to pose them an impossible task! What a powerful physical (of course, not only physical) change has taken place in this relatively short time between first and eighth grades.

How we work with the child during the first seven years of life is important, because the physical body is the foundation on which the subtler human bodies build. The physical body is also the basis for the human "I" to achieve self-awareness. Immediately here we can ask the question: If the body is not developed in a proper way, what is the impact on the much -needed healthy self-consciousness and self-assurance of the child? The physical brain makes it possible for the etheric life-and-forming body to create mental images. The physical body supplies the astral body with a basis for feeling by way of the rhythmic system. Our awareness of the physical body enables the "I", our eternal essence, to experience itself as the central core of the human being. Our thoughts, feelings, and actions need the physical body in order that we may have conscious experiences in earthly life. In addition, we need our senses so that the "I" can take in the world and organize our perceptions. Our experiences here in the earthly environment depend on our healthy physical body. Therefore, the care of the physical body is of preeminent importance, especially in the first seven years of life when it is still being cast into the necessary and healthy forms.

Steiner elaborates the physiological point of view: "Every part of the body involved in the activity of the metabolic system is directly connected with human will. The circulatory or rhythmic system forms the physiological basis for the human feeling, and the nerves-senses system is immediately connected with thinking and the life of conscious ideation."[10]

To observe in the young child how thinking awakens through physical activity, through the will, can be a delightful experience. A first grader totally engaged with beeswax modeling suddenly shouts out full of amazement, "Look, teacher, what I made: a snail!" Only after seeing the end result did the thought wake up in him to what his hands had created. In moments like this we clearly see how acting in the world awakens thinking. On the other hand, we might observe a handwork lesson in a seventh grade, and we immediately realize from the students' questions that everything first needs to be carefully explained before the work can begin. Here again, we marvel at the inner transformation that takes place between ages seven and fourteen, literally a movement from the limbs to the head.

When we observe the body in the middle grades, especially from ages nine to twelve when rhythm, repetition, breathing, and artistic activity are so essential, we see that the middle, the chest area of the developing human being grows, expands, and is elaborated. We see how physical growth moves from the head (in ages 0-7) to the rhythmic system (especially ages 9-12) and down into the metabolic and limb system (at 14-15 years). We see how this system now becomes the focus, how the limbs grow and become strong. This is especially visible with the boys. It can astonish a person to notice the size of the shoes of eighth grade boys lined up outside the eurythmy room! It is often in the course of the sixth grade when teachers notice many other changes, particularly visible in their faces. Nose, mouth, and chin become more chiseled, and more individualized. What we see here are the physical manifestations of an overall soul transformation taking place.

Rudolf Steiner encouraged the teachers to be aware of each subtle change in the way the students carry their body; for instance, how this changes between ages seven and fourteen. In addition, he made them aware of something we generally don't think about. He asked the teachers to notice that while they are teaching, the students are actively growing and changing physically–and to understand that with their teaching they must not disturb the child's growth, for this would affect how the physical body will develop. As Steiner explains in *Study of Man*, "The child has to grow…and while educating him you should realize that he must grow rightly. What does this mean? It means that you must not by your teaching, by your education, disturb the child's growth…your teaching and education should only be such as is compatible with the child's growth. What I am now saying is of special significance for the primary school period. For just as up to the change of teeth there takes place the building up of forms from the head, so during the primary school period – from the change of teeth to adolescence – there takes place life-development, growth and all that goes with it. Life development which proceeds from the chest, only reaches completion with the onset of adolescence."[11] Steiner points out here that fixed hardened concepts affect the child's growth and life forces, hardening the fluidity of these forces.

As Waldorf teachers, we need to be aware that before the change of teeth in the children, a stream of forces works from the head downward. These are forming forces. They form the organs and the whole body. After the change of teeth we are dealing with a stream of life forces. Here the focus shifts from physical to etheric life body. Breathing and circulation are connected with the middle system, with life. If there is a mood of stress or fear in the classroom, it works adversely on healthy breathing and circulation rhythms. Adults basically have a four-to-one rhythm of breathing (pulse rate to breath) that establishes itself between the ages of twelve and fourteen. Stress or fear in the classroom affects the rhythmic system and may incline the child towards asthma. A warm, harmonious atmosphere is a necessity for learning; as teachers we can stimulate these physiological processes either in a positive or in a negative way.

The etheric body -- life, vitality, and form

When we speak about life, vitality, and form forces, we speak of our etheric forces or etheric body. This subtle body works closely together with the physical body, and as a matter of fact never leaves it during life on earth. The etheric body shapes and forms the physical. In *The Education of the Child*, Rudolf Steiner describes it in this way:

> Now beyond the physical body spiritual science recognizes a second essential principle in the human being. It is the life body or etheric body...For those who have developed the higher organs of perception, the etheric or life body is an object of perception and not merely an intellectual deduction...Human beings have this etheric or life-body in common with plants and animals. The life-body works in a formative way on the substances and forces of the physical body and thus brings about the phenomena of growth, reproduction, and inner movement of vital body fluids. It is therefore the builder and shaper of the physical body, its inhabitant and architect. The physical body may even be spoken of as an image or expression of the life body. In human beings the two are nearly–though by no means totally–equal in form and size. The etheric body is a force-form; it consists of active forces, and not of matter.[12]

We experience the etheric body and its forces in its growing, healing, and regenerating capacities, and also in our level of energy and vitality. In short, its forces keep our physical body alive, energetic, and functioning. Looking at the body from the physical perspective, we are aware that when the etheric life forces withdraw at death, very quickly disintegration sets in. Our etheric body needs to remain closely bound up with our physical body to keep it alive.

In addition, we need to consider that the etheric body is the bearer of our more permanent tendencies in life. It is the bearer of our character, talents, and temperament, also of habits and inclinations, of our compassion and memory.

The care and strengthening of the children's etheric forces should be a high priority for the teacher, especially during the time when it is most accessible, from six to seven years of age onward.

How can we work in a healing and strengthening way on the etheric life body? We can do this by working on the mood and the social climate in the class, by establishing a good rhythm in our lesson with thorough repetition, along with developing good habits. (For example, finish the work at hand before starting a new project!). The arts of form drawing, modeling, and eurythmy strengthen the life and forming forces. The story material in every grade, including the pedagogical and nature stories, and seating the children by temperament address the etheric body. For a healthy etheric it is important to establish moods of reverence, gratitude, and awe in the classroom. Beyond that the teacher should ask herself: How is my speech? Is it monotonous, too fast, does it lack flow, does it sound like information? How is the pitch of my voice? Too high? All of this affects the life sense of the students. Heart-warmth and inner joy, and for the home environment religious practice (any religion, as Steiner emphasized) lift the etheric because they focus heart and soul on something higher than what is experienced in the everyday. The artistic element and story material open the soul to the world and lay a foundation of healthy morality and compassion. What enters the etheric body remains available for a long time. The etheric is our time body, the keeper of memories life-long.

Age-specific needs for etheric health

We need to study life forces also from another perspective. Steiner opened up a different and totally new perspective with his groundbreaking discovery of the metamorphosis of the life-and-forming forces into thought forces during the first seven years of life: "It is of the greatest importance to know," he says, "that the human being's ordinary forces of thinking are refined form and growth forces."[13]

Why is this discovery important? Because it brings into view the reciprocal relationship between the life and health forces in the body and our thinking activity. We can reflect on the connection between the quality of thinking, for instance, and physical health. The teacher can bear in mind that when something has a negative effect on the life forces in the body, like tiredness, stress, over-stimulation, illness, and so on, it will also affect the ability to think. Conversely, erroneous, scattered, illogical thinking will have a negative effect on physical health. Many questions can arise from these considerations. For instance, what consequences on our and the children's physical health can we expect when thinking deteriorates to mere information gathering? We certainly are approaching that time rapidly, if we have not already arrived.

Consequently, the Waldorf Main Lesson (and all other lessons) should have a clear, logical, underlying sequence and structure. The children do not need to know this, but they can *feel* it. Having this underlying clarity in everything the teacher presents is a "must," for it reinforces the child's (and the teacher's) etheric forces and models clarity of thought.

When we engage in thinking, in contemplative activity, we now realize that in this activity we meet the life forces in their *body-free* form. Thinking is an invisible activity, invisible for our earthly sense perception; it is an inner activity. We can experience it because we are doing the thinking. To engage in contemplative thinking is essential for human beings. It is an activity that lets us withdraw from the world; it gives us distance from the objects in our environment, so that we can observe and distinguish them more precisely. Thinking also gives us the much-needed distance from ourselves. For a healthy social life and interaction, we need to have self-awareness and self-knowledge.

In lecture seven of *Study of Man,* Steiner brings an important point, important for the teacher herself as well as for the children: Children need to learn to separate their feeling from their doing, otherwise they will remain impulsive, acting out of momentary feelings and emotions, rather than thoughtfully

25

considering what they do. If children never learn to separate their feeling from their actions, they will have a difficult time as adults to volunteer to do something just because it needs to be done. They will tend to go by whether they feel like engaging or not. Determining what to do based solely on one's feeling is an egoistic tendency; it poses a challenge when working within groups later on in life. Steiner makes it clear that as we mature, feeling needs to unite with thinking. As it does, gradually thinking gains the warmth and compassion that make it possible to consider others and feel for them. As an adult we can then step out of the habit of seeing ourselves as the center of the universe. This experience is truly healthy.

The ability to see ourselves from a distance is helpful, for instance, in faculty meetings. We gain perspective on the fact that our ideas are not always the only good ones that absolutely must be implemented. When emotions rise in meetings, thinking brings in reasoning that cools the flares of emotion and calms volatile situations.

Dr. Michaela Gloeckler, head of the worldwide Anthroposophic medical work, elaborates Steiner's extraordinary discovery, offering us further understanding of the importance of his discovery:

> It was an extraordinary discovery by Rudolf Steiner that the life forces and the thinking forces are identical. When they are working within the physical body, they are life forces, when they work in a body-free condition, they are our thinking and conceptual life. We need to contemplate this concept: life is incarnated thinking and thinking is excarnated life. It is important to recognize this double nature of life, incarnated life works in time and space and excarnated life is beyond time and space, and gives us an experience of eternity. It is out of this sphere that the teacher has to study the subjects that he wants to teach. When a teacher engages the child on the level of physical activity, be it sports, eurythmy, form or geometric drawing, writing, in short, all non-verbal activities, he is working with the incarnating forces of the etheric. When engaging the child's

thinking, he works with the excarnating etheric forces. As we pointed out earlier: all activities affect the child in health or illness. So do these activities.

Too much incarnating activity undermines the age-specific loosening of the etheric forming-and-growth forces from the body. Then the transformation into thought-forming activity will not be harmonious. Therefore, the whole Waldorf curriculum must be age-specific. It is not oriented to how capable or challenged the child is in academic abilities. We teach certain things at a certain age. The teacher needs to meet the age-specific needs and find ways that every child can participate in at least some aspects of what he or she brings in teaching. So, the curriculum is a specific balance between incarnating and excarnating activities.[14]

A healthy breathing between world and self is necessary. And if the ego is actively engaged during the day taking things in with interest, the after-effect is that the life of the etheric forces is strengthened and enhanced. The etheric forces can then bring regenerative powers into the physical organism. When there is little self-engagement, little active, attentive participation, or perhaps emotionally aggressive, destructive behavior, or a bombardment of sense impressions, the after-effect will be negative and destructive to the vitality of the organism.

During the day, the etheric forces are divided; they work on the one hand in the body and on the other in thinking. There is the conscious thought life and the subconscious life activity in the physical organism. The conscious thought life receives impressions from the world and thinks them over.

During sleep, the conscious (mental) and subconscious etheric (life) forces work as one, in unison again since we have no consciousness during sleep time. All of the etheric forces are given over to the regeneration of the life processes in the physical organism. How well this regeneration can be accomplished depends very much on what children take in during the day. When a child receives healthy, nourishing pictures, then the etheric regenerative forces are strengthened. This will have a life-enhancing after-effect. However, if the daytime hours are spent in front of the computer with video games, movies, and other screen entertainment, the etheric forces are assaulted, which has a negative, even destructive effect on the vitality of the whole organism. To have a clear understanding of this is an enormous support for the teacher. Ideally, the teacher will know enough about the home-life of her students and will be sure to adjust her instruction, focusing at times perhaps exceptionally strongly on certain health-supporting activities.

In the classroom we can strengthen the etheric forces of the children in many ways. Already mentioned as essential were the warm, positive classroom atmosphere and the teacher's relationship with her students. If the teacher works in a heart-warmed way, the students feel held and carried by her. The teacher's love for the subject matter stimulates and motivates the students, while the rhythmic flow of the lesson and the daily repetition in the sequence of the Main Lesson give a sense of security. The images that the teacher brings and the whole moral underpinning of the lesson with its artistic execution fill the child with a sense of meaning and purpose. Both reverence and devotion are moral-religious elements and are sources of inner nourishment, strength-giving for the etheric.

During the day the etheric forces are divided –
on one hand they work in the body, on the other in thinking.

Day – time

Conscious thought-life

Body-free activity

Unconscious life of body

Body-oriented activity of
the ether-body

Night – time

Unconscious regenerative
life of the body

Whole body oriented
homogenous activity of
the etheric body

During sleep the conscious (mental) and
subconscious life-forces work together.

The astral body--rhythm and relationships

We now approach the second subtle body of the human being. The physical body is a material body, clearly visible. The etheric body, as we learned, is our life body. When we look at our soul, our inner space, then we speak of our astral body or our astral forces. Rudolf Steiner describes the astral body in this way:

> The third member of the human body is called the sentient or astral body. It is the vehicle of pain and pleasure, of impulse, craving, passion, and so on…the astral or sentient body is a figure of inwardly moving, colored, and luminous pictures. The astral body deviates in both size and shape from the physical body. In human beings it presents an elongated ovoid form in which the physical and etheric bodies are embedded. It projects beyond them – a vivid, luminous figure – on every side.[15]

The astral body has as its physical basis the rhythmic system. Its gesture is in-breathing and out-breathing. In the first lecture of *Study of Man*, Steiner discusses the importance of breathing in its many aspects. In one sense breathing forms the essential bridge between child and world and between child and other human beings. Physically, breathing connects us with the environment around us. And we can say that no astral body is healthy unless it feels itself to be connected with the world and other human beings. The astral is the body of relationships.

Having a strong sense of connectedness, having good relationships, gives the child health and security. Says Dr. Michaela Gloeckler, "The key to the wellness of our astral body is the healthy breathing between world and self and in our various relationships. Resiliency research, an aspect of Salutogenesis,[16] points to a third factor beyond heredity and environment that is crucial for human physical health: human relationships."[17]

That relationships influence health and an individual's resiliency in coping with problems makes sense. So in the classroom, a harmonious, joyful relationship between teacher and students is crucial. A child's interest and motivation to learn depend on this loving and genuine relationship. Becoming healthy and whole includes a process of integration that needs to happen in the classroom. When a child feels isolated, not accepted, sidelined, it is a cause for illness. Each child must experience that she or he is part of the class, included in all activities, loved and appreciated.

Dr. Gloeckler elaborates on the meaning of good relationships because they are a source for physical and psychological good health for all of us:

> We actually have three essential elements that we can focus on to ensure the 'good' quality of a relationship: interest, honesty, and respect. These are high moral values, and they were crucial to Steiner. It is the relationship that builds a bridge to carry the teaching to the student; it flows from heart to heart. When these three moral qualities are at the core of the teacher's ethics, then the child can feel and intuit the teacher's integrity. And when a child has experienced even one good relationship when growing up in an unhealthy environment, this still makes it possible for her to develop in a healthy direction in her life.[18]

We can feel these words spoken directly to us as teachers.

Our emotional and feeling life, our astral forces, have quite a different quality from our thought life. We can align our thoughts clearly and logically. We can think in pictures that have continuity. We can make sense of things. Our feelings, however, can be unsteady. They come and go, and may change from one moment to the next. Yet, mature and purified feelings can be sensitive organs of perception. We can use them to assess and judge situations. With them we can "read" what is needed. We certainly do not like to have mixed feelings; they make us uneasy, indecisive, and hesitant.

Whereas our etheric forces are our sculptural-pictorial forces, the astral forces are the musical-poetic forces.[19] Our astral body, then, is also a body of music. We can imagine relationships consisting of musical elements that sound out of the reciprocal give and take between people. Our astral body or soul produces melodies that change their arrangements and moods constantly as we take in and respond to other human beings, to nature, and to our environment. Rudolf Steiner often draws the teachers' attention to this musical astral body: "The astral body itself, in its true inner being and function… can only be comprehended by understanding music – not just externally, but inwardly…The only thing that is earthly about the astral body is time, the musical measure. Rhythm and melody work directly out of the cosmos, and the astral body consists of rhythm and melody."[20]

We could even say our soul is pure music, perhaps particularly evident between the ages of nine and fifteen when the emotional life of the teenager begins to sound forth. And music itself plays a major role in harmonizing the incoming astral forces. Of course, music nourishes our soul throughout life. At the time of adolescence, however, quality music has the power to bring a palpable harmony into the classroom. This harmony is felt in the soul as relief, a freeing, an expansion – all feelings that are helpful when young people are struggling with inner disharmony, emotional ups and downs, and awkwardness in the body (affecting boys particularly).

The teacher can do much in the years starting with grades four or five to harmonize the incoming astral, emotional forces by engaging the students in playing quality music. Regular music instruction is of great value as is an orchestra for the middle school as well as the high school. In addition, it is rewarding for the class teacher from fifth grade upward to change the first fifteen to twenty minutes of Main Lesson from a focus on outer, physical movement to inner, soul movement, which, as we heard, is musical. Then also the teacher is addressing the shift taking place in child development in these middle grades, from a focus on doing (will) to an emphasis on feeling, the rhythmic system.

Between teacher and faculty, and teacher and child, there is a constant flow of feelings, and learning takes place within and by means of this stream. Steiner pointed out early on that feelings and emotions have a powerful role in stimulating learning. Therefore, Waldorf education directs all learning to engage the feeling and will life in the lower grades, and these are guided to awaken gradually the thought life. When the teacher takes this path through feeling, it affects thinking. Thinking then develops with compassion, and by way of willing, thinking also will remain practical and connected to reality.

The "I" being--the ego and transformation

Every human being has a fourth member as part of his being, and that is the "I", the ego, the Self. The "I" is solely a human dimension. It is revealed and finds expression in our very own path through life, our individual biography. The class teacher can be fascinated by seeing the individual qualities and faculties of the children emerge more and more through the years. Yes, individual aspects are visible already in kindergarten, but to have (hopefully) eight years as class teacher to experience the sacred unfolding of the individual is awe inspiring.

We sense the holy mystery of the human being when Rudolf Steiner says that "the name "I" can never reach my ear as a description of myself….With the "I", the "God," who in lower creatures reveals himself only externally in the phenomena of the surrounding world, begins to speak internally."[21] Then he adds, somewhat enigmatically, "The vehicle of this faculty of saying "I", of the *I-faculty*, is the *body of the I*, the fourth member of the human being."

The "I" is the transforming agent in the human being. It connects with and enters into all other subtle members of the human being and develops them. How do I experience the "I"? When I concentrate on what I do and am fully present in it, then I am; I create out of my center. When I concentrate like that, then there is no room for stress or hectic energy. I become stressed when I lose myself. As long as I realize myself as "I" and am active in the present, concentrated, giving myself direction, then I remain calm, inwardly centered, and at the same time active. Then I am connected to myself.

The signature of stress is lack of initiative, unrest, agitation, inner insecurity that can increase to fear. Fear is always an indication of the absence of the "I". One way we can strengthen the presence of our "I" as teachers and adults is by working with exercises that school attention, such as the six essential exercises given by Rudolf Steiner as practices beneficial for all adults. Attention is an "I" activity.[22]

Furthermore, what we *do* shows who we are. Initiative and interest are "I" capacities, as well. The "I" is always in the here and now, in the present. The "I" is fresh, open, taking in, responding. Everything that enters into our consciousness enters through the "I". We can also be on overload because of too much input. Then the "I" is circumvented. This is the case when technologically-produced images encroach on the individual soul in rapid-fire fashion. They allow no time for the "I" to connect and thus weaken its activity. Images then enter into the human being below the threshold of consciousness. By this means images are not digested, not thought through, not questioned. And yet these images take up residence in us.

The "I" is strengthened by continuity in relationships when they are healthy, meaning built on trust, honesty, and appreciation of the other. During and after puberty, the "I" is strengthened by ideals, by common goals, by a supportive working together. We also strengthen the "I" when we strengthen the activity of the will. Later on, taking on responsibility, being dependable when carrying out assignments is a sign of the "I" taking hold.

The "I" engages in two polar activities: one activity is that of complete identification, complete engagement with something we do, for example, an artistic activity, in which we unite with it so strongly that we completely forget about ourselves. The other activity is that of separation. We can distance ourselves from an activity or from someone; we withdraw into ourselves to ponder, contemplate, and gain understanding. The "I" is an active, form-giving force in us. We can call it the "manager" of our whole being. It is the thinker and the planner.

When the "I" lives in the body, it is anchored through cognition in the nerve-sense system, through feeling in the rhythmic system, and through willing in the metabolic and limb system. The "I" gives form to our whole being, down to the physical, and brings form into the entire journey of our life. According to Rudolf Steiner, the "I" is a gift from high spiritual beings called the Spirits of Form.

In the course of child development the "I" penetrates the part of the human being that becomes free, or "has been born," as Steiner often puts it. We can see in the chart below how the "I" takes hold of the bodies during the seven-year developmental periods of the child:

Ages	Body in which the "I" works	What the "I" does
0-7	"I" works in the physical body	schooling it, forming it, by way of the child's imitative capacities. It develops the will.
7-14	"I" enters the etheric body	partially freed from the physical body. It develops thinking and memory.
14-21	"I" works in the astral body	partially freed from life body (physical and etheric) beginning at 12-14. It develops the feeling life.
21-28	"I" in the "I"-carrier	"I"-carrier (all subtle bodies) has established itself and the "I" can enter into it.

Again, we experience the "I" activity in two different ways: on the one hand, in the ability to identify with and merge with an activity. On the other hand, we can pull back, find our own center, distance ourselves from our doing, in order to observe what we have done and how well we did it. Even though we have these two activities of the "I", the identifying and the distancing capacity, the "I" itself is the *indivisible* Self that is our undivided and eternal core.

Rudolf Steiner explains that while we can distinguish our four bodies, we cannot completely separate them, for they interweave: "These four components are entirely different from each other, but ordinary observation does not distinguish between them because they play into one another. Ordinary observation never goes so far as to recognize the revelation of human nature in the etheric body, the astral body, or the ego. But it is not really possible to teach and educate without knowledge of these things."[23]

Each subtle body or member of the human being manifests through a different activity on the physical level:

- The "I" *integrates*
- The astral *differentiates*
- The etheric *proliferates*
- The physical *isolates*

These are the activities of the four human members. The "I" integrates and harmonizes. It has the overview. The astral differentiates. It says: the hand needs five fingers, the foot needs five toes. We can also say: the astral counts. The etheric grows and proliferates. Through the physical body, we experience ourselves as separate individuals.

The metamorphosis of the growth forces into thought forces brings to expression the double nature of the human subtle bodies. They build up the body and give it form and structure on the physical level, differentiate it on the etheric and astral levels, and work in an integrative way via the ego organization.

Human development and the role of imitation

As educators we have the joy of guiding children. They change and transform. Therefore, a detailed knowledge and understanding of human development must be added to our knowledge of the human being and the subtle bodies.

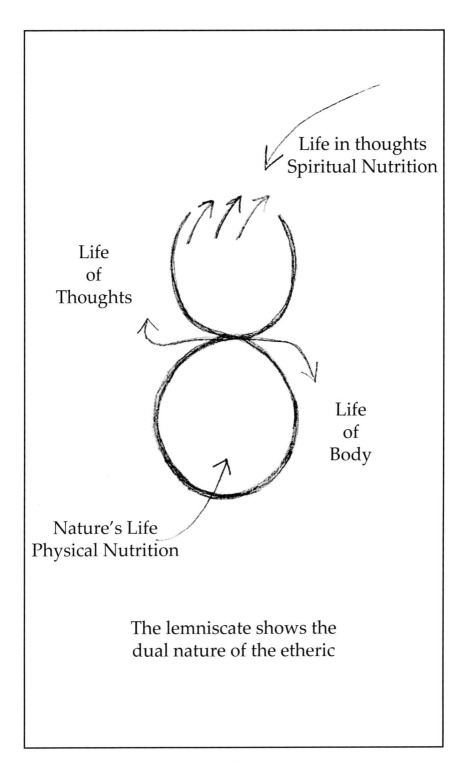

Life in thoughts
Spiritual Nutrition

Life
of
Thoughts

Life
of
Body

Nature's Life
Physical Nutrition

The lemniscate shows the
dual nature of the etheric

Steiner speaks of a birthing process. Each body is born and becomes accessible to the individual. However, the bodies are born at different ages. The first birth occurs when the physical body frees itself from the protected environment of the mother's womb. The physical body is then ready to be exposed, gently though at first, to temperature, air, sound, to breathing and digesting, and gradually also to perceiving. Caring for the health and well being of the physical body needs to be our focus, especially during the first seven years of life before the change of teeth, when this body is still in the early processes of being formed. The physical body makes human incarnation possible, makes thinking, feeling and acting possible here on earth. The body must be attended to properly so it can fulfill these essential tasks.

The importance of physical development is why in Waldorf education we make sure that the life and forming forces working in the physical are not siphoned off by engaging them too early in academic learning. We know well that it can easily be done. However, it will show itself later on in adult life in various physical weaknesses or even illnesses. Early on, the child's entire system is extremely impressionable. All that he experiences in his environment has an effect on his body. Says Rudolf Steiner,

> The child is like a sense organ. The surrounding impressions ripple, echo and sound through the whole organism because the child is not so inwardly bound up with its body as is the case in later life, but lives in the environment with its freed spiritual and soul nature...the spirit, soul, and body of a small child are still undifferentiated, still interwoven as a unified whole. The soul and spirit work in the body and directly influence the circulatory and digestive processes. It is remarkable how close a child's soul and metabolism are to each other, and how closely they work together. Only later at the change of teeth does the soul element become differentiated from the metabolism. Every stimulation of a child's soul is transcribed in the blood circulation, breathing, and diges-

tion. This means that a child's environment affects a child's whole body.[24]

Before the change of the teeth, children imitate what they see. Through imitation, impressions become habits and skills. Memory at this time of life is not about inner pictures but about habits and skills. Little children move and play, acting out all they have seen, heard, and felt in their environment.

In early childhood appropriate stimulation of the senses and free play are essential for healthy development. Play needs to be spontaneous and free without interference or instructions from adults, so that the acting out and trying out can actually occur. It is at this time, then, that sensory integration problems and motor disturbances can be spotted and addressed. The teacher must realize that it is only in these first seven years that the etheric, astral, and ego can be reached and addressed through activities of the physical body. How the teacher engages the body through meaningful movement, through artistic activities, crafts, puppetry, practical work, setting the table, sweeping the floor, and so on affects and develops all the bodies, not only the physical body.

Imitation is a powerful learning tool during approximately the first seven years of life. When, after that time, the bodily intelligence begins to free itself to work as thought activity, the imitative capacity dwindles.

> The later ability of abstract thinking is transformed motor ability: When you teach a four-year old to ride a bike, you do not only train his body but also his thinking ability, because at that point the thought forces are not yet freed from the body, they are still connected with it. The other forces remaining in the body nourish only the organs so that they can continue to work throughout life...The freed forming forces, on the other hand, are now outside the body, forming our thoughts...We can think a lot of nonsense but luckily the body does not form itself accordingly.[25]

In der ersten Hälfte unseres Lebens bemühen wir
die ältere Generation zu verstehen,
in der zweiten die jüngere.

weller-mode.ch
Muttenz

Imitation is a powerful learning tool.

We can begin to understand: Thinking activity is body free. Life activity in the body of the child (growth, regeneration, health) is the biologically manifesting thought life. Life is biological intelligence.

Educating before and after the change of teeth

At six or seven years of age when the second dentition is taking place, the etheric body is birthed, meaning its forces become accessible to the child and may be used for forming thoughts and concepts as the soul space of the child begins to develop. Now the etheric forming forces enable the first grader to bring much clearer form to memories. As the etheric forming forces strengthen the "I" activity, the child can bring up these memories at will, an activity necessary for academic learning. This is a powerful development in capacity. Teachers may notice that children now can hold on to their memories purely through inner activity; they do not need physical objects as outer props that were still necessary at ages three to four. Now, remembering becomes a soul-spiritual activity.

Teachers benefit enormously from reading about child development before and after the age of seven from as many different sides as possible. Steiner speaks about it often and from varying perspectives. Through what he says a teacher can obtain a full picture of this momentous transformation occurring in the child. Because Steiner's remarks appear in so many different lectures, I have collected here a number of his remarks on this topic for my readers' easy access. I encourage teachers to mark this section for future reference and study.

During the early years, the soul and spiritual life of the child is completely connected to the physical and organic processes, and all of the physical and organic processes have a soul and spiritual quality. All of the shaping and forming of the body at that age is conducted from the head downward. This stage concludes when the second teeth are being pushed through. At this time, the forces working in the head cease to predominate while soul and spiritual activities enter the lower regions of the body–the rhythmic activities of the heart and breath. Previously, these forces, as they worked especially in the formation of the child's brain, were also flowing down into the rest of the organism, shaping and molding and entering directly into the physical substances of the body. Here they gave rise to physical processes.[26]

Steiner makes us aware here that the forming of the child's physical body is brought about by forces streaming downward from the head. That is the direction of physical forming seen in embryology; the head is formed first, then the chest, then the limbs. Later the forming forces develop the soul. On the physical level the shift is at that time to the rhythmic system, which serves as a physical manifestation of the soul life.

Some of these forces begin to work more in the child's soul and spiritual realm affecting especially the rhythmic movement of heart and lungs. They are no longer as active in the physical processes themselves, but now they also work in the rhythms of breathing and blood circulation. One can see this physically as the child's breathing and pulse become noticeably stronger during this time. Children now have the strong desire to experience the emerging life of soul and spirit on waves of rhythm and beat within the body - quite subconsciously, of course.[27]

Of the many ways in which Steiner approaches the seven-year change here follows a physiological view:

Through the change in the working of children's ether body, the limbs begin to grow rapidly, and the life of the muscles and bones, including the entire skeleton, begins to play a dominant role. The life of muscles and bones tries to become attuned to the rhythms of breathing and blood circulation. At this stage, children's muscles vibrate in sympathy with the rhythms of breathing and blood circulation. Previously, the child's inborn activities were like those of a sculptor, but now an inner musician begins to work, albeit beyond the child's consciousness. It is essential for teachers to realize that, when a child enters class one, they are dealing with a natural, though unconscious, musician. One must meet these inner needs of children, demanding a somewhat similar treatment, metaphorically, to that of a new violin responding to a violinist, adapting itself to the musician's characteristic pattern of sound waves. Through ill treatment, a violin may be ruined forever. But in the case of the living human organism, it is possible to plant principles that are harmful to growth, which increase and develop until they eventually ruin a person's entire life.[28]

In another lecture Steiner discusses the emancipation of intelligence from the body, and the ego or "I" taking hold of it:

What we call the birth of the etheric or formative force body can also be seen as the emancipation of the intelligence from the physical body, a two-sided description of the same phenomenon. We can grasp the matter only by observing two such aspects at the same time. In spiritual science nothing can be characterized without approaching something from different sides and then combining the different aspects in one comprehensive view...In this period, therefore, an intermingling takes place between the eternal ego and the slowly liberated intelligence...But again it is the ego, the eternal element that unites itself with what is being freed, so that from birth to puberty...we have a continuous anchoring of the ego in the entire human organization. After the seventh year, the ego settles itself only into the etheric body, whereas previously, while the human being was still an imitator – indeed due precisely to this imitative activity – it worked itself into the physical body, and later, after puberty, it worked itself into the astral body. What we have then is a continuous penetration of the human organization by the ego.[29]

With the change of teeth children enter a new relationship to the world, and they first need support in this meeting of the world.

As the life of their own soul gradually emerges, which they now experience in its own right, they must first meet the world supported through an experience of authority. At this stage, educators represent the larger world, and children have to meet it through the eyes of their teachers. Therefore we would say that, from birth to the change of teeth, children have an instinctive tendency to imitate, and from the change of teeth to puberty, they need to experience the principle of authority. When we say "authority," however, we mean children's natural response to a teacher – never enforced authority. The kind of authority that, by intangible means, creates the right rapport between child and teacher.[30]

Here Steiner points to the fact that children from age seven to ages twelve or thirteen need guidance. They search for someone to emulate, someone who has become an author of his or her own life, an authority, who has confidence and self-assurance and can lead the students in that time period into a healthy connection with the world and with other human beings. This means an adult not caught up anymore in the reactive mode of the teenage years but someone who has found their "I", their inner moral-spiritual essence. Such an individual thinks, ponders, verifies and only after that acts in full consciousness.

Here Rudolf Steiner speaks about the seven-year periods as continuing throughout life:

One can recognize such seven-year periods throughout the entire course of human life, and each of these periods falls into three clearly differentiated shorter periods. If we observe the gradual withdrawal of some of these etheric forces until approximately the seventh year, we can see that in the first two-and-a-half years after physical birth the etheric body frees itself from the head region, how in the following two-and-a-half years it frees itself from the chest region and finally, up to the change of teeth, from the child's metabolic and limb system. Thus we can recognize three phases within the gradual withdrawal of etheric forces.[31]

The imitative capacity of the young child is an expression of the living intelligence of the body. It was already active when the body, this awe-inspiring vessel that we each received, was formed for this earthly incarnation. As mentioned before, this capacity to imitate (to know through *inner* identification with) decreases when thinking and memory begin as soul capacities.

> To summarize, before the change of teeth, children are not yet aware of their separate identity and consequently cannot appreciate the characteristic nature of others, whose gestures, manners of speaking, and even sentiments they imitate in an imponderable way. Up to the seventh year, children cannot yet differentiate between what lives in them and in another person. They experience others as directly connected with them, similar to the way they feel their own arms and legs... With the change of teeth new soul forces of feeling, linked to breathing and blood circulation, come into their own, with the result that children begin to distance themselves from others, whom they now experience as individuals...Their previous inclination was to imitate the more external features, but this changes after the second dentition. True to the nature of children, a strong feeling for authority begins to develop...But this sense for authority in children between the change of teeth and puberty must be respected and nurtured, because it represents an inborn need at this age.[32]

The unfolding human development, as we have seen, is a beautiful and sacred thing. As Waldorf class teachers, we are midwife to this sacred unfolding of the child's individuality as it reveals itself more and more with healthy, life-filled education. Waldorf education takes the inner being of each person into consideration and understands its task to be the reverent holding and nurturing of this inner being.

Building memory before and after age seven

Rudolf Steiner speaks in *Study of Man* of remembering and forgetting as a fundamental ability of human soul life. He points to its rhythm as an activity engaging the "I". Similarly, the rhythm of waking and sleeping is an activity of the astral body. Both rhythms are a kind of breathing. Remembering is essential for the continuity of our identity experience, for holding together our personality. On the other hand, it is a blessing to be able to forget, to let go so we have room to take new things in. It is pathological not to be able to forget.

We think, feel, and will day in and day out, transforming what we take in into memories. This treasure of memories makes life into a connected whole. As human beings we comprehend new learning by linking it to the content already gathered in our memory. Rudolf Steiner says a great deal about this subject.

> Through the ability of the soul to retain our daily experiences, it turns the outer world into its own inner world. It retains the outer world through memory. Thus life becomes a lasting consequence of the transitory impressions made by the outer world.[33]

> Remembering means being able to visualize something anew; it does not mean that a mental image can come to life again... Remembering means...linking a past experience to my present life. The soul imprints on the body the process by which something becomes a memory. However, the soul must first do the imprinting, and then perceive its imprint just as it perceives something outside itself.[34]

> The will takes hold of a mental picture down in the unconscious and raises it into consciousness...only by working through the force of habit can you give order to the will and therewith also to his memory.[35]

Memory is linked with the metabolic system, connected to the will.

> The spirit transformed its treasure trove of memories into abilities. No experience is wasted; the soul preserves each one as memory.[36]

When we focus on the ability of the younger child to remember, we may notice how closely memory is linked to the changes occurring in the physical body and soul body around the age of seven. We recall that up to the change of teeth all human members–the etheric, astral and "I"–work together in building up and forming the physical vessel. This work takes place in the child below the threshold of consciousness. With the freeing of the forming forces from the body, thoughts and memory get a boost; they become clearer because they are now more formed. Memory is stronger and can now be activated at will. Steiner puts it this way:

> The power of memory which works in the soul-spiritual is nothing else than the transformed, metamorphosed force of growth; and to develop the forces of growth and nourishment is just the same, albeit on a different level,...[than it is to] cultivate memory, the power of recollection. It is the same force, but in a different stage of metamorphosis...During the first years of a child's life both these forces are merged into one another, they have not yet separated; later on memory separates from this state of fusion and becomes a power in itself, and the same holds good for the power of growth and nourishment. The small child still needs the forces which later develop memory in order that he may digest milk, and the stomach be able to carry out its functions; this is why he cannot remember anything. Later, when the power of memory is no longer the servant of the stomach...then part of the forces of growth are transformed into a quality of soul, into memory, the power of recollection.[37]

Since, as we mentioned above, all members of the child work together on the physical body from birth to six or seven, and the etheric has not yet separated off to become active in thinking and memory, it would be premature to engage children in academic learning. Memory should be left alone to develop naturally, at least until five years of age. To draw away the forces too soon from their work on the physical can have consequences for the health and well-being of the children:

> Till the age of five, let memory develop naturally – do not force intellectual learning and demand mem-

orization of letters and numbers. This fosters later in life rheumatism; rather, foster the child's fantasy and imagination.[38]

Out of a child's imitative actions, the soul develops skillfulness, which permeates the child's finer and more delicate organization. A child will imitate something one day, and then do the same thing again the next day and the next; this activity is performed outwardly, but also–and importantly–within the innermost parts of the physical body. This forms the basis for memory in the early years. After the change of teeth, memory is very different because by then... spirit and soul are freed from the body, and picture content can arise that relates to what was experience in the soul...The small child does not yet produce these inward pictures...prior to the age of seven, children live in their habits, which are not inwardly visualized in this way.[39]

The memory in the early years is based on habit. There is no internal visualization until the separation of the etheric from the body. Memory is based on doing actions repeatedly.

A child's memory differs before the change of teeth and after. Before the second dentition memory is habit, it is bound to the activities of the body, imitating actions, repeating them again and again, this forms the basis for memory in the early years...Only when we view children from this perspective do we see the radical and far-reaching changes that occur with the coming of the second teeth.[40]

After the seven-year change memory works in a new way in the child; it is, as we have seen, a soul-spiritual activity forming images in the soul that are remembered as mental images. The child before the change of teeth does not form inner pictures. Back at the age of about three and four, the child uses outer objects for play and overlays these with his imagination and fantasy. The object (like a table) can become whatever it needs to be for the moment: a restaurant scene, a lion's den when a blanket is thrown over it, a train with chairs on top, or a plane. It can also become the counter of a store. Absolutely anything is possible. Fantasy and imagination do their part.

There is an even earlier form of memory that we can see in the very young child. We can call it place or local memory. Something has to be physically present to jog the memory. Markers and monuments used to be erected at the roadside, and when people passed by these markers, they would recall the event. Memory was not yet within, but without, and memory awakened when passing such a marker. We experience the presence of this memory also in the young child, when recalling grandma's house only when again in front of it!

Memory needs to be left alone up to the change of teeth, for what the child acquires during this time through imitation and sense perception stimulates the forces of will underlying the development of memory. During these early years we should not interfere, but let the underlying forces strengthen.

We can experience a second stage in this early habit memory when children pass from what we called the *local* memory to *rhythmic* memory. In pre-history, we see this in the oral tradition during the time of the great epics in different parts of the world. Memory then was carried by the rhythms of the verses sung or recited by bards while the people gathered to listen to their treasure of stories that connected them with the spiritual roots of their peoples.

The young child goes through this stage beginning around four years of age, when he loves to hear the same songs and same little rhymes over and over again and cannot get enough of them. The rhyming helps the memory also.

> [When] the element of soul-and-spirit is released from the body in a certain sense, systematic training of the memory is of the greatest importance. Through the whole of a man's life the memory makes claims on his physical body. Unless there is an all-round development of the physical body, the memory will be impaired in some way...An undue development of memory will injure the child for the whole of life.[41]

What is an "undue development of memory?" Steiner points here to an overtaxing of the memory with intellectual theoretical concepts: "Above all we must realize that abstract concepts–concepts built up by the rationalizing intellect–are always a load on the memory, specially in the period of life between the change of teeth and puberty."[42] Even at that later seven-year period, seven to fourteen, intellectual abstract concepts tax memory. What then are the things that enliven and strengthen the memory during that time of life between the change of teeth and puberty: rhythmic, artistic activities and imaginative pictures. "Given vividly in an artistic teaching, [they] awaken living forces which play right down into the physical body and which allow the memory to unfold in the right way. The very best foundation for the development of memory is to give our teaching in an artistic way during the elementary school age."[43]

Steiner gives us three golden rules to support the development of memory:

- Intellectual concepts overload the memory

- Artistic activities enliven and build it up

- Will activities strengthen it and make it firm

This is a fantastic guide for the teacher when the question is asked, "How will the children remember?" Steiner also encourages the teachers to notice when children turn pale for this could be too much of an exertion of memory: "Growing pale and paler is the result of overexertion of the memory and must be relieved, whereas in the case of a child with excessive color, we must set about developing the memory."[44] After age seven the child has the ability to form a body-free picture content; for example, when listening to stories in grade one, they can recall the stories and retell episodes. This ability is connected with the changes occurring in the etheric body. Remembering is now more precise, and recall happens at will.

Steiner strongly suggests that until the age of puberty many treasures should be gathered by the child and stored in memory. Intellectual understanding should definitely follow later. Reasoning is a soul force that only awakens from puberty on, meaning through the ability of the astral body, and should therefore not be employed before the birth of this subtle body. However, memory development is connected with the shaping of the etheric body. We could say, when teaching history, for example, first they should assimilate historical events (using biographies) through memory (collecting treasures) and only later comprehend them in intellectual concepts.

> Until puberty children should be storing in their memories the treasures of thought on which humankind has pondered; later intellectual understanding may penetrate what has already been well imprinted in memory during the earlier years. It is necessary for human beings to remember not only what they already understand, but to come to understand what they already know–that is, what they have acquired by memory...The more children know in memory before they begin to understand through intellectual concepts the better.[45]

What Steiner brings in the above quote challenges our present day conceptions. We feel that we have to explain everything, so that the child understands. If we do this, we teach to the intellect. Steiner, on the other hand, makes us aware that until puberty children should be storing treasures in their memory and later come to an understanding. Understanding will be fuller, richer, more meaningful and satisfying, when we work in this way.

As teachers we always have the whole life of our students in mind. Steiner explains that what the child experiences at the beginning of life has consequences towards the middle and end of life:

> Our etheric body is a time-body, and what happens at one time is not lost, but appears later in life in changed form! When we look in that way at the whole life, then we will understand that diabetes can be the consequence of the time between the change of teeth and puberty–the memory was overtaxed, overbur-

dened, used and perhaps abused with tests and fear and stress. How you work with memory at a certain time will later show its consequences in the metabolism, at the age between 35 and 45. Those things that have remained in the soul, that have not been digested from overloading the memory, cause rheumatism or diabetes.[46]

Between the ages of nine and twelve a child's feeling is integrated into the gradually awakening cognitive activity. To nurture the feelings and support them securely, the student needs to experience that the world is beautiful. This feeling then enters into his perceptions. Perceiving is in those years still an artistic, creative process, not yet a process of systematized thinking that experiences an objective world. Feelings for the past and the future begin to play a role; at nine more focused on the past, at age twelve the future opens up. This opening brings a new and greater perspective to the student in these middle years. The element of feeling has a strengthening effect on the ability to remember, not only at this time in life but throughout.

Steiner draws the teacher's attention to the significant role feeling plays in remembering. Today this role is widely acknowledged: "Today it is scientifically proven, that emotions play a decisive role in the formation of memory. The limbic system is responsible for this."[47]

Around ages twelve to fourteen abstract memory develops, connected with the astral body. The causal thinking awakens, connected with the bodily experience of the hardened bone. Harmonious movement now becomes bony and edgy, even awkward, as the transition is taken to conceptual thinking. We want the students now to observe carefully when the teacher performs a science demonstration in front of the class. It becomes clear to the teacher very quickly how challenging it still is for some of the sixth graders to recall the lawful sequence of the proceedings.

Weakness of memory is a weakness of will in the thought life. To increase will in thinking and assist focus and concentration, we can ask students to look intensely at things and then look away and tell us what they remember with as much detail as possible.

Will and feeling are strengthened in the etheric through reverence, devotion, gratitude, wonder, awe, contentment, peacefulness, and harmony within, as well as truthfulness, integrity, and transparency in the social life. We weaken the etheric through suspicion, doubt, lack of clarity, lack of transparency, and untruth. Good habits always help memory.

Vivid interest makes memory strong and efficient!

Understanding loneliness at the nine-year change

The seven-year cycles in human development can be further subdivided into three time periods. According to Rudolf Steiner, like the first seven-year period, the second seven years, from ages seven to fourteen, also "fall into three smaller phases. The first lasts from the change of teeth until approximately the end of the ninth year; the second roughly until the end of the twelfth year; and the third from the thirteen year until sexual maturity."[48]

The nine-year change separates the child from his natural experience of connectedness (this separation can, of course, be forced on the child earlier), awakening the ability to distance himself as from the environment in order to observe it. The nine-year-old begins to realize that there is a separate, inner space developing in which secrets can be kept out of sight! However, this also means experiencing being alone, a loneliness that can come with a subconscious realization of standing at an abyss that yawns between self and world. This experience comes with the child's developing subject-object consciousness. The "I" enters into the feeling life and senses the loss of oneness, the loss of connection also with the spiritual world. At this age, the developing self-experience begins to drive out the previous faint but still present awareness of spiritual reality. These delicate inner experiences may be lost considerably earlier than age nine for children in today's world, with its brutally noisy, garish entertainment. Children may even not be able to develop their spiritual connections in the first place.

The author, Hermann Hesse, recalls his life between nine and twelve very sensitively. He articulates a fine inner sense for what the child experiences and shares creative interpretations of a child's imagination. First, he writes about his world as a young child:

His World as a Young Child

There were many things and connections which only existed for me and in me. Nothing was so mysterious, so

The earth is my home.

When a child undergoes the nine-year change, a good connection with life needs to be established to gain security and confidence.

outside of all daily routine, and yet nothing was so real as my world…A well-known chair or stool, a shadow by the stove, the crinkle in the newspaper could become beautiful, ugly or evil, important or insignificant, luring or inhibiting, laughable or sad. How little was stable, hardened, and permanent! Everything was alive, changing, metamorphosing, longing for dissolution and rebirth!

What a beautiful picture of what goes on in the world of the child. He then recalls the different inner experiences as he neared age twelve:

Near the Age of Twelve

Now every month, every day led me closer to fixed goals. Everything pointed in one direction; everything led me away from the play and the presence of my previous days, which had not been without meaning, but without a goal, without a future. My wish and dream to become a magician stayed with me, but it began to lose its power. It had enemies, something opposed this dream and this was real and undeniable. Slowly, slowly, slowly the blossom faded. Slowly something limited approached my unlimited previous world. It was the real world, the world of the adults…Now the vast thousand-fold world of possibilities was limited, fields divided, parted by fences. Slowly the jungle of my days changed, the paradise around me solidified. I did not remain what I had been, prince or king in the land of possibilities. I did not become a magician, I learned Greek… Imperceptibly the magic evaporated all around. The wonderful story in my grandfather's book was still beautiful, but it had a page number which I knew and there the story was today, tomorrow and at any hour. There was no more miracle… Everywhere the magic fled, much became narrow that once was wide, much became poor, that once was precious.[49]

Bruno Walter, world-renowned conductor, also remembers that crucial time of childhood:

> I see the place before me where I experienced something like an inner trembling of my whole being, like a melancholy awe. I do not remember how I came to be alone on the school yard–anyhow, I entered the yard, which I previously had only known filled with the noise of playing and romping children. It seemed to me, therefore, twice as empty and lonely. I see myself standing there overcome by the deep silence, and while I listened to the silence and to the lightly blowing breeze, I felt something approaching me from somewhere out of this solitude. It was something unknown, something powerful gripped my heart. It was my first inkling that I was an individual, my first notion that I had a soul and that something called to it – from somewhere.[50]

The philosopher, Karl Jaspers, remembers the sense of loss:

> I was ten years old. An overwhelming feeling of loneliness came over me, although I was yet a child. It was like experiencing a great loss. At the same time I sensed that an infinite abundance was waiting for me. This made my soul wide while at the same time it seemed to want to break my heart.[51]

The descriptions of Herman Hesse, author, Bruno Walter, composer, and Karl Jaspers, philosopher, raises into our consciousness how essential it is for children this age to have time alone to hear the voice from eternity calling to the soul. Children's time is often filled with activities, with things to do, driving here and there for this and that to fill their time. Children whose lives are overly busy may miss out on essential experiences that could open totally different dimensions to them and bring awareness and meaning into their life.

I am an "I". I am an individual. I am powerful.
I can give direction to my life.

In grade three, a Waldorf class teacher can realize with gratitude how perfectly the Waldorf curriculum addresses the feeling of separation and loneliness at the time of the nine-year change. This new soul condition, the subject-object consciousness, also brings feelings of insecurity, perhaps even fear. The child needs strengthening. Every third grade Waldorf teacher gets to experience how the practical activities in the curriculum are welcomed with enthusiasm by the students and how these subjects bring inner strength and consolidation to the child's soul life. It is exciting to observe how dramatically the third-grade activities of house-building, cooking, sewing, and gardening change the students. Their self-confidence grows almost daily, and visibly!

This dramatic change can also be seen in the children's musical experiences during these three different phases between the ages of seven and fourteen:

> If you observe the way children live entirely within a musical element, you can understand how these three phases differ from one another. During the first phase, approximately until the end of the ninth year, children want to experience everything that comes toward them in relation to their own inner rhythms–everything associated with beat and measure. They relate everything to the rhythms of breath and heartbeat beat… Until the ninth year, children have a strong desire to experience inwardly everything they encounter as beat and rhythm. When children of this age hear music… they vibrate with the music, reproducing within what they perceive from without…Before this, through imitation, rhythm and beat directly affected the formation of bodily organs. After the change of teeth, this is transformed into an inner musical element.[52]

The teacher can address this longing for rhythm and beat also during circle time at the beginning of Main Lesson. This can really be addressed with active movement during the first three grades. Here we can expand the musical experience to speech and let the students feel the rhythm of the verses, poems, and songs.

Steiner gives us a clear picture here of how music in the early years affects the forming of the physical bodily organs directly and then, in the second seven years, moves into the soul, to become an inner movement that forms the feeling and thinking soul. This can really bring to the teacher's consciousness how important it is in the early years what kind of music surrounds the young child and similarly how important it is to introduce students to quality music from the moment they begin to learn to play an instrument in Waldorf schools. After the age of nine and up to twelve, music is a more separate experience coming from outside, and now, as Rudolf Steiner explains, the young person can approach it through thinking also:

> On completion of the ninth year and up to the twelfth year, children develop an understanding of rhythm and beat and what belongs to melody as such. They no longer have the same urge to reproduce inwardly everything in this realm, but now they begin to perceive it as something outside…This continues until the twelfth year, not just with music, but everything coming to meet them from outside. Towards the twelfth year, perhaps a little earlier, children develop the ability to lead the elements of rhythm and beat into the thinking realm, whereas they previously experienced this only in imagination.[53]

At this age, then, they can understand, count, and experience the different rhythms, can learn notation, and can use this knowledge in their own compositions.

At age 7-14 music becomes an inner soul movement
and forms the feeling and thinking soul.

The birth of the astral body follows usually from ages eleven to thirteen in our present time. This means that the feeling life that has freed itself from the dependence on the physical body becomes more and more individualized due to the awakening thinking, due to the wish to think things through. Now the young people can withdraw more easily into their own soul life than the younger children whose astral body and consequently their feeling life are still bound to the physical and etheric bodies. At this time they swing between sympathy and antipathy. Likes and dislikes shoot forth as purely emotional manifestations. The calming and clarifying guidance of the "I" is not yet sufficiently present to take hold of these emotions. It penetrates them only gradually. The calming element of thinking that the "I" brings has to be added and modeled by the teacher. At this age, the teacher should be the natural authority for the child, the benevolent authority.

Toward the twelfth year the sixth graders want to lift their experience more into the realm of abstract and conscious understanding:

> And this coincides with the hardening of those parts of the muscles that lead into the tendons. Whereas previously all movement was oriented more toward the muscles themselves, now it is oriented toward the tendons. Everything that occurs in the realm of soul and spirit affects the physical realm. This inclusion of the life of the tendons, as the link between muscle and bone, is the external, physical sign that a child is sailing out of a feeling approach to rhythm and beat into what belongs to the realm of logic, which is devoid of rhythm and beat.[54]

Working with these three steps in the development between ages seven and fourteen, we come to the realization that movement first connects and uses the *muscle*, then addresses itself to the *tendons*, and finally addresses itself to *bone* and uses it. In this last phase of the more-pronounced experience of the bony nature, the young person can develop abstract thinking and reasoning.

When we come to the time between eighteen and twenty-one, physical growth ceases for the most part, and on the soul level a certain maturity sets in, which includes the ability to take on responsibility. This is possible because the organizing principle, the "I" principle, is born. The human "I" itself has a nature of will, of intention. It has the capacity to be the great integrator. Thinking, feeling, and willing have freed themselves from the body and the young person feels he or she can be in charge of life and take on responsibility. At times this may still be more of a wish than a reality. But clearly, there is a level of maturity that can be for parents as well as for the young adults themselves a long-awaited joy and delight: to be able to take hold of the will and guide it with conscious determination.

Contemplating this whole process of freeing thinking, feeling, and acting from the body can fill us with awe. Through this freeing process it is possible for an individual to become conscious, independent, and morally responsible. The freeing of the etheric forces makes individual thinking possible, the freeing of the astral forces makes individual feeling possible, and the freeing of the "I" organization makes possible free will activity. We can feel deep gratitude as human beings when we recognize the profound wisdom manifesting in human development.

In a child between ages seven and fourteen, we are dealing with the soul of the child and the interplay of thinking, feeling, and will activity, and says Rudolf Steiner, if we "can thoroughly understand the play of thinking, feeling and will–in the soul's life–…we have a basis for the whole education."[55]

Rudolf Steiner described the human being as threefold–physiologically, psychologically, and spiritually. We are therefore always dealing with three levels on which the threefoldness appears.

Physiologically:

Nerve-Sense System	Rhythmic System	Metabolic-Limb System

Psychologically:

Thinking	Feeling	Willing

Spiritually:

Waking	Dreaming	Sleeping

Rudolf Steiner explains this threefoldness of the human being further, saying:

> his thinking is entirely bound up physically with the nerve senses system of his organism, his feeling is bound up with the rhythmic system, particularly the breathing and circulation system, and that his will is bound up with the system of movement and metabolism. The development of these three systems is not alike. Throughout the different epochs of life they develop in different ways.[56]

Waldorf teachers are aware that the three systems need constant attention and nourishment to assure their healthy development. Teachers learn to address these systems on each of the three levels. When we write them down as shown above, they lend themselves to the much-needed meditative contemplation. We need to let this live in us: Bring before you the various ways these threefold systems interrelate, support one another, and work together. It is helpful to work with the above in a self-directed way, coming up again and again with our own elaboration of each, so that we can experience what our own level of understanding is. Then, also bring before you the way they relate to each other and work together at the different stages of child development. This understanding and elaboration is key for the teachers' heart connection with the children. This is how the "imponderables" that Steiner speaks of as a connecting thread between pupil and teacher, are built up.

These indications are a much needed help for the teacher when pondering how the whole human being is addressed in a healthy way.

For a healthy *"I"* the activity is:	*attention,* focus, identification, and truthfulness
For a healthy *astral* body the key is:	*interest,* empathy, universal love, and supportive relationships
For a healthy *etheric* body we need:	*reverence,* devotion, respect, and gratitude
For a healthy *physical* body:	*care of the senses,* healthy rhythm, movement, and nutrition

From the above indications the teacher can glean what each member of the human being needs to develop optimally.

The role of mood as motivator

Steiner brings teachers to an awareness of "imponderables" that weave between them and their students. For a healthy learning atmosphere there needs to be harmony between teacher and students. The mood in the classroom is of paramount importance. It is the glue that holds it all together. Furthermore, the students need to experience that the teacher is engaged with her feelings in the subjects she teaches. When they are aware of the teacher's interest and enthusiasm, the students can feel drawn into the subject and motivated to explore the subject further. Moods create feeling responses, and it is clear from research done in recent years that learning happens best–should only happen–when it occurs with positive feelings.

The preeminent role feelings and emotions play in learning is confirmed by current research. Manfred Spitzer, a well-known brain researcher in Europe, says, "The role of emotions in learning can hardly be overestimated."[57]

Research shows that neutral material is stored in different parts of the brain, depending upon the emotional condition in which the learning took place.

> Learning in a positive emotional context stores words successfully in the hippocampus, while learning in a negative emotional environment is stored in the amygdala…the function of the amygdala is associated with fright and flight and this condition is called forth in the body during recall of the material… When the amygdala becomes active, pulse and blood pressure increase, and muscles tense up…From all this follows: If we want our children and young people to learn in school, then one thing must be right: the emotional atmosphere during learning. We now do not only know that learning occurs optimally when in a good mood, but we know now *why learning should only happen when in a good mood.* For then only, can what is learned be used later to solve problems![58]

Rudolf Steiner had already seen beyond Spitzer's assertion above by pointing out that feeling fosters will activity in a natural way, and that is why feeling is a strong motivator: "What is feeling really? A feeling is very closely related to will. I may even say that will is only the accomplished feeling, and feeling is will in reserve. Will which does not yet express itself, which remains behind in the soul, that is feeling: feeling is like blunted will."[59]

Feeling is the great motivator of the will to engage the child. Enthusiasm works wonders. Negative feelings can kill any activity.

That is also why continual emotional distress can create deficits in a child's intellectual abilities, crippling the capacity to learn. Harmony between teacher and students helps eliminate emotional distress. Students want to experience that they matter to the teacher, that the teacher sees them, that the teacher is interested in each one. If they feel ignored, sidelined, overlooked, or, worse, disliked, then not only do they lose confidence, but the harm done may continue to haunt individuals for the rest of their life. Daniel Goleman, psychologist and science journalist, speaks to the role of emotions in his book, *Emotional Intelligence,* saying, "Emotional aptitude is a meta-ability, determining how well we can use whatever other skills we have, including our intellect."[60]

We can be amazed that Rudolf Steiner emphasized the importance of feeling for learning already at the beginning of the twentieth century.

Another aspect that will affect the feeling life of the students and their motivation in the classroom concerns the teacher herself. How does she feel about herself? Is she at peace with herself, centered, confident, positive, and affirming of life? This can be seen in posture, engagement, and smile, in the lightness and joy of soul, in the clarity and uprightness of the spirit.

These aspects of the teacher's character are easily gleaned by students of any age, more or less consciously. We have the familiar saying: Actions speak louder than words. Particularly teachers need to remember that.

The teacher's main task

The harmonizing and integrating of our whole being is one of the lifelong tasks that challenge all of us every day of our existence. When a child is born into this earthly world, harmonious integration is essential, and it needs to be accomplished in the child's own being.

Two very different entities must find their way together for a human being to be born. One part descends from the spiritual world, the other has been prepared through generations, through heredity. The first part is the spirit and soul (the spiritual, individual reincarnating essence) and the other is the living body (coming through heredity). These two entities need to connect in a rhythmically balanced way so that the individual gifts (and challenges) that the child brings with him from a previous life can be integrated with the hereditary biological gifts and shortcomings. They need to work together in a karmically fulfilling way. This is of major importance for the health and the well-being of the incarnating child. When the child is born, his soul-spiritual individuality and hereditary body both make life on earth possible. They need to learn to interact and work in a balanced way together. What a task!

Rudolf Steiner brings this task to the teacher's consciousness in the *Study of Man.* There he has a great surprise in store for the Waldorf teacher when he elaborates the spiritual understanding of the teacher's task. Her greater task is not what we might assume, that is, to teach subjects and skills. Steiner reveals something entirely different; namely, to bring the soul and spirit that have entered the child at birth into harmony with the living body: "They must come into harmony with one another...for when the child is born into the physical world, they do not as yet fit one another."[61] Clearly, this harmonious integration is a process that continues over a number of years. Also, immediately after the *Study of Man* lecture, Steiner addressed the theme of this integration again in *Practical Advice to Teachers*:

> Above all, we have to realize that...we shall be dealing...with the harmonizing of...the human spirit and soul, with the physical, bodily human...The subjects you teach will not be treated in the way they have been dealt with hitherto...What matters for you will *not* be the transmitting of knowledge as such; you will be concerned with handling the knowledge for the purpose of developing human capacities.[62] [emphasis by author].

How is that possible? The task of the Waldorf teacher then clearly is to assist in this process of rhythmic interpenetration of the two different entities, so that the child can grow up into a balanced individual. Both the soul-spirit and the living body must find expression. A beginning teacher asks; "How on earth am I supposed to do that?" Steiner does not leave us hanging here, he immediately continues, "Let us now consider this task more concretely," and he goes on to speak about the breathing process and its importance for the human relationship to the world and to other human beings.

Somewhat later he even proceeds to the greater breathing of "sleeping and waking," the day and night rhythm.[63]

The etheric body and physical body are closely connected throughout life, day and night. They are the human bodies (members) that stay in bed when we sleep. The "soul and spirit" part, the astral body and the "I", leave the body and connect during sleep with the moral spirit world, their home, and, on awakening, bring back forces of rejuvenation that both the physical and etheric bodies need. Humans are both earthly and spiritual beings. When we wake up, the astral and ego connect with the body again. The ego and astral body, however, are only loosely connected with the etheric and physical bodies in the early years of childhood. The astral body uses the breathing process to connect rhythmically with the etheric and physical bodies. In-breathing, the astral body connects, out-breathing it loosens. We can say we breathe our eternal being out and we breathe it in again.

After birth this connection remains tentative, and occurs only briefly during the few waking hours of the infant. Gradually, though, the connection strengthens. For the eternal being of the child needs to make a good connection with the physical body. It will be his garment and should be the best possible tool for him to fulfill his task in this earthly life.

The child not incarnated enough

The harmonious connection can fail in two directions. On the one hand, the soul and spirit may not connect well enough with the body, remaining outside, instead of taking proper hold of the physical vessel to penetrate it in a healthy way. Not making a sound connection may have as a consequence a lack of awakeness, lack of sensory engagement, a tendency to remain dreamy, perhaps even withdrawn, and in their own world. Children in this situation may drift away easily, lost in their own thoughts or imaginative picturing (depending on the age). They do not take hold of their environment enough, nor engage actively with their senses. In class they may miss part of the instruction because they are not sufficiently attentive. However, they may listen well when stories are told, or participate in artistic activities, especially drawing and painting.

Artistic work is ideal for a dreamy child. It invites the child to connect gradually and warmly with his or her body and with the environment. It is not the stark or shocking element, but the artistic and imaginative that speaks to this child. Storytelling stimulates children to picture inwardly. Here we also see what a blessing it is for the dreamy children to begin their learning process with story and drawing when letters are introduced. Nature stories, created by the teacher, are an effective way to connect the child with his natural environment.

Knitting assists dexterity and incarnates the child.

Any art or craft using the hands, bringing attention to the work of the hands, is already an incarnating process. Writing or drawing with their feet will bring their attention (attention is an "I" activity) all the way down to their feet. We also have the child experience the times tables with his whole body through rhythmic movement and counting, through clapping and stamping and other activities with his limbs.

In addition, tasks in the classroom such as watering the plants, sweeping the floor, washing the counters, emptying the trash, and so on are excellent challenges for the child not sufficiently incarnated to have to remember and carry out. All these examples are ways to help him become more attentive to his environment and experience his own physical body in a natural and non-disturbing way. If we do not succeed to connect this child, we could later have an individual withdrawn from the world, socially inactive. Perhaps the person is full of great ideas and suggestions but sadly not able to bring these down into his will and manifest them as activity in practical life. Such an individual may lack the ability to "take hold of" his will in order to guide it toward a practical goal. The soul-spirit needs to be invited to connect with the body in a healthy, balanced way.

I have chosen here to stay with the child not incarnated enough as an example of a child that remains relatively disconnected from healthy integration with the physical body. There are, of course, other reasons why the soul and spirit might be less firmly incarnated. We may see this in any form of Asperger and Autism disorders. Another reason why a child would shy away from coming into a good connection with the body would be any kind of shock experiences in early life.

The child too deeply incarnated

The second way a harmonious connection can fail to come about is when the soul and spirit are drawn too deeply into the physical body, in which the physical body and physical environment becomes the sole focus and soul and spirit are ignored or denied. The effect of this could even be that the soul-spirit becomes bound, even imprisoned in the body. Interest then swings toward what the physical senses and the physical, man-made world has to offer. The tendency here is to become too awake too early and too materialistic.

A teacher who notices this tendency in a student would focus in this case on loosening the soul and spirit by bringing the inner being into activity; we are speaking about the soul. The soul is pure music. This gives us a strong hint about what to do, in what direction to go. *Music would be a means to loosen this soul from the chains of the body.*

Many class teachers have fruitful experiences using music, singing, and rhythmic work at the beginning of Main Lesson.

Especially in the middle and upper grades when students are already quite capable in playing recorders (alto, tenor, soprano), the beginning of Main Lesson is a great time for them to play together. The students usually approach this with great enthusiasm and joy. Furthermore, beginning the day with music follows Steiner's indications that the *outer movement* of the lower grades should be changed to *inner movement* in the middle grades. Inner movement is music, and if healthy music, such as folk music from around the world, minuets and so on is introduced, it can assist in loosening the tightly connected body and soul by helping the child toward more inner and outer flexibility. Also, through the flow of the rhythm in any piece of music, healthy breathing can establish itself again between soul and body, and the soul begins to sing again. In addition, watercolor painting is an activity that lends itself well to the loosening of the soul. In watercolor painting, nothing is fixed and hardened. For this child it will be a help to bring "magic" back into life. Stories, too, with rich pictures and descriptions will promote loosening and inner flexibility.

It is the Waldorf teacher's task in the middle and upper grades to lead the child or young person into the world. Interest in all aspects of nature through the various sciences leads students into an understanding of the world around them.

By making use of drawing, for example in a botany or other science classes, the teacher can develop and hone the student's ability to observe keenly and carefully. This attention will connect them with the world, which is an out-breathing. In the upper grades by asking them to ponder and then draw conclusions about what they saw, smelled or heard; we ask them to become inwardly active in thought, we let them breathe in. This is one example of how the teacher always has to be aware in any subject of bringing the soul-spirit in and then leading it out into a connection with the world again. The dreamer needs to become attentive and awake to the outer world through the artistic activities and through this stimulate the stronger use of the senses.

In the middle grades the young person needs to gain a healthy connection with the world.

Healthy movement activities, preferably also eurythmy, handwork, and woodwork (which awakens children through the resistance of the wood) are actually good for both dreamy children and those too awake. It is clear, though, that students too tightly connected with their body, and prone to focus on the outer material world, need to become active in their inner realm. It is the Waldorf teacher who has to make sure that the eternal part, the "I", is not "captured" by the body, is not pulled in too deeply into the physical. A healthy breathing between the soul-spirit and the living body is the goal the teacher hopes to achieve.

The restless child

I would like to point out something I came upon when reading "Overcoming Nervousness." In this lecture Rudolf Steiner points to causes for nervousness, we may speak of it now as restlessness:

> The physical body is normally the servant of the etheric body, and that in turn has to be directed by the astral body. If not directed by the astral body, the physical body executes movements on its own; it is symptomatic of an unhealthy condition. These jerks represent the subordination of the etheric to the physical body, and denote that the weak etheric body is no longer fully able to direct the physical…Here the physical body has become dominant and makes movements on its own, whereas in a healthy human all his movements are subordinate to the will of the astral body working through the etheric.[64]

I was amazed at this understanding of nervousness, which is insight into what today may be called *attention deficit disorder*. Jorgen Smit, Waldorf teacher, speaker, and author of numerous books on education and spiritual development, and a member of the Executive Council of the Anthroposophical Society, elaborates on Steiner's insight:

> When you fall out of the time-organism, then nervousness begins. Nervousness starts also for other reasons.

When the I simply lets all soul-forces go unhindered, unchecked, all thoughts, feelings, wishes, drives, desires, just lets them go, does not take hold of anything, then the astral body becomes weak, grows limp. What does 'limp' signify? The astral body has a great fullness but when the I does not send its impulses into it, does not work in it, the astral body grows weak, limp. What are the consequences? Then the astral body cannot inspire the etheric body anymore, and now the ether body also becomes weak, meaning susceptible to outer influences, allergic. When we have allergies it is a certain weakness to outer influences. The stronger you are, the less allergies do you need to battle. The weak etheric body loses its grip on the physical, and now the physical 'falls out,' separates to a certain extent…Not completely, or you would die.[65]

When the physical body disconnects from the other bodies, nervousness arises, showing itself in motor unrest, nervous ticks. The physical body fidgets. It is not held nor guided by the subtle bodies. The opposite process begins when the "I" takes hold of the soul forces, which includes the drives and desires, and checks them, containing them and guiding them toward something productive, humanizing them. When the "I" takes hold, nervousness lessens or may even cease, for the "I" brings direction. This will certainly not be a process happening overnight! Smit continues:

The moment we, as teachers, can guide the feeling and willing of the children into a healthy direction, the astral body becomes stronger. Then the astral body can inspire the etheric body more effectively, and the ether body then is less prone towards allergies. It is stronger and can take hold better of the physical body, ordering it and healing it.[66]

Here we are made aware that when the spirit loses its guidance of the life and physical body, the physical body begins to fidget. Rudolf Steiner connects health and healing to the spiritual resources of individuals; health comes from spiritual wellsprings beyond the threshold. As adults we need to access these sources consciously through our own efforts. Children need their teachers to be aware of these interactions. I mentioned before that everything a teacher does, how she thinks, feels, and acts, affects the students. The younger the children, the more directly they are affected.

When the class teacher makes a continuous effort through the years to recognize the eternal individuality of the student struggling to connect here on earth with the given physical body, the student feels welcomed into life, into this time, and into the community. By inwardly holding a picture of the student's true inner potential, the teacher enables this potential to be sensed and gradually taken hold of by the student. A simple verse addresses the situation and can be used by the teacher, especially in middle grades:

> Within my heart's an image
>
> Of all that I should be,
>
> Until I have become it
>
> I never shall be free.
>
> Anonymous

Part II

Practical classroom work: the role of rhythm and pictures in teaching

Appreciating the twelve senses

In turning to practical classroom work, the teacher needs to understand how to cultivate the senses for healthy development. How a child can best take hold of his body in the first years of life depends a great deal on the healthy integration and diverse use of his senses. He needs to have bodily experiences that help him incarnate securely and connect well with the hereditary body.

The development of the senses is a central concern in Waldorf education. Children can be impeded in their healthy sensory development if they lack certain primary sense experiences. A well-differentiated schooling of the senses is the basis for both the bodily and the soul health.

Teachers and parents need to remain aware how deeply affected children are by their surroundings. "The child is like a sense-organ," says Rudolf Steiner. "Surrounding impressions ripple, echo, and sound through the whole organism because the child is not so inwardly bound up with its body as is the case in later life, but lives in the environment with its freer spiritual and soul nature. Hence the child is receptive to all the impressions coming from the environment."[67]

The children's sensitivity to the environment is particularly acute during their first seven years.

> Until the change of teeth children are essentially one sense organ, unconsciously reproducing outer sensory impressions as most sense organs do. Children live, above all, by imitation...Insofar as very young children inwardly reproduce all they perceive, especially the people around them, they are like one great, unconscious sense organ. But the images reproduced inwardly do not remain mere images, since they also act as forces, even physically forming and shaping them.[68]

In Waldorf education, teachers educate with an awareness not only of the five traditional senses of sight, hearing, touch, smell, and taste but of the twelve senses described by Rudolf Steiner. The human "I" connects with the impressions received in such great variety through the twelve senses to understand the world. Also, using the twelve senses enables the teacher to expand and refine the descriptive images that she brings to the children in story and history material. Through descriptive sense experiences the content of the images becomes more alive for the children and a more palpable experience.

The twelve senses:

Upper senses, or knowledge senses	
The sense of:	the Other or (Ego sense)
	Thought
	Speech
	Hearing
Middle senses, or feeling senses	
The sense of:	Warmth
	Sight
	Taste
	Smell
Lower senses, or will senses	
The sense of:	Balance
	Movement
	Life
	Touch

The four lower senses

The four lower senses, or the will senses, play a major role in early childhood. They are fundamental in order for the child to develop trust and security. Rooted in the physical body, they enable the child to have experiences in relation to the outer world that tell him about the condition of his physical body. Is it in movement? Is it in balance? Is it well? Steiner points to these bodily will senses as the necessary foundation for the healthy development of the higher-knowledge senses that make human social life possible. While human beings are only dimly aware of these bodily senses, they govern the child's incarnation process, affecting whether it will be sound or unsound.

The sense of touch gives the child a gentle body awareness through the experience of coming up against boundaries. The child learns where the self ends and the world begins. In a sense the child is always inwardly touching its body, which makes the body feel like home and develops a feeling of security in the child. He feels safe in his own body and in his environment. A healthy sense of touch develops trust in the world and in others. We are also constantly in touch with spiritual reality. So, the sense of touch also makes awareness of the divine possible.

As class teacher, we can ask ourselves: How do I foster the experience of touch? Do I have enough materials available in the classroom to give many different tactile experiences? It is good to go over the lessons and become conscious of the touch experiences they provide. This can be an eye-opener for the teacher!

In the Waldorf kindergarten teachers develop a keen awareness of the children's interactions with natural materials of all kinds, from prickly pine cones to soft silks, from thick sheepskins to delicate little shells, from nut shells to wools, and so on. When children enjoy free play, they find plenty of opportunities to handle different objects and materials. Preparation of the warm meal in the kindergarten engages the children in cutting vegetables, setting the table, pouring the drinking water, and kneading the dough for baking. Having a wide range of experiences sensitizes and refines the sense of touch, readying it for the time when it frees itself from the bodily experiences and becomes a powerful asset for social life. The metamorphosed sense of touch allows the child to have a multifaceted as well as sensitive perception of the other person; it becomes the sense for perceiving the inner being of the other.

The sense of life makes us aware of our bodily constitution. We sense our well-being, our general state of health, our vitality and energy, our *joie de vivre*, our inner organic harmony. Do I feel full of life or am I tired, getting sick, exhausted? Am I hungry, thirsty? We experience the condition of our etheric body in its interaction with the physical. Our entire physical body is an organ of perception for the sense of life.

The young child needs to find a good relationship to his body. He needs to feel well in it, develop a sense of identity with it, feel comfortable and secure in it. To feel "at home" in oneself is fundamental for the whole life. How we feel about the world, how confident we are, has a great deal to do with how comfortable we feel within ourselves. Our sense of self has a direct connection with how well we are incarnated in our body.

In play the child feels comfortable and secure.

In the early grades, a positive, warm mood in the classroom speaks to the sense of life. So does the lightness and joy of the teacher. The breathing between the parts of the Main Lesson, the rhythmic return of verses and songs, the movement activities every morning, the familiar progression of activities through the day, all these relax the child and give him confidence.

Questions for the teacher regarding this sense could be: Is learning interesting and engaging for the children? Is the lesson presented in a way that the child can enter into it, meaning, are there enough images that build a bridge for the child to connect with the subject matter?

Outside the classroom a child might be exposed to sensory overload, or experience a breakdown in family life, face a hectic, non-stop lifestyle, be rushed from one activity to another all week long. These experiences stress and damage a child's sense of well-being and harm his much-needed feeling of security. The teacher would need to talk with the parents about the harmful effects of such situations.

The sense of movement is actually a perception of self-movement. We sense when we are out of balance, when we are about to fall, when we are standing straight and upright. Are we in control of our movements?

Movement is an expression of personality. Our actions, and how we go about achieving them, reveal who we are. How do we act and how does the world react to us? When we work with others, can we flow with the ideas presented, or do we bristle at everything that we cannot agree with? Can we feel the movement in our own life and are we aware of its transformative power as we evolve? Our inner movement comes to expression in our biography, our path through life. Our body and soul movement, the experience of growth and maturing, calls forth our feeling of freedom. But we also experience it when our life begins to stagnate, when we become too fixed, for then there is little or no movement and no experience of freedom!

A sign of our times is a chronic movement deficit. Children struggle with obesity, posture problems, and weak muscle tone. Therefore, this sense that perceives movement needs our particular care and attention.

Movement development cannot be separated from sense-development. It stimulates the growth of synaptic connections in the brain. The richer and more differentiated the sense impressions, the greater the complexity that manifests in the networking of the central nervous systems, and, in addition, the more diverse will be the sensory motor spectrum that will be available to the individual throughout his life.

Since the discovery of the mirror neurons, it has become clear that humans inwardly imitate every movement they see, the younger the more intensely this occurs (see page 108). This gives parents and teachers pause to think: What kind of movements do I want my child to imitate? What is healthy movement that expands the child's talents and abilities (sewing, knitting, modeling, drawing, and so on)? What are movements I would not want my child to do over and over? (Think of media intake and the violent actions on some video games.)

In the classroom the teacher needs to be aware of the flow and rhythm of the lesson, the movement in each activity. The Main Lesson rhythmic part or circle time introduces the child to ensouled, meaningful movement. The teacher incorporates gestures and movements into poems, verses, and songs. These are rhythmic and ensouled movements, movements that inspire from inside out.

We can understand why Steiner brought eurythmy as a healing element into Waldorf education. In eurythmy the child can hear the soul "sing" through the movements. Form drawing is also a completely new and unique activity; its movement of lines has a stimulating and vitalizing effect on the etheric life forces, activating them even during sleep when the etheric body is more active, when a redoing and perfecting of forms is an ongoing activity.

At the opposite pole, teachers cannot escape noticing the increase of restlessness and inner agitation in a good number of children. This lack of inner stillness may come from an inability to calm the motor system, to put it to rest. Consequently, the child cannot focus, listen, nor internalize the material presented sufficiently. Bringing the movement organization to rest is a precondition for learning. Therefore, the teacher needs to develop an awareness of when her students have been sitting too long. Interjecting activities into the two-hour Main Lesson to get them up and moving, is of great help. In addition, a few children might benefit from doing gardening for a half hour, even during Main Lesson, or from engaging in some therapeutic eurythmy exercises, or working with a remedial teacher.

The sense of balance orients us to the world. Its organ is the semi-circular canals in the ear that stand ninety degrees to each other. Through the sense of balance we experience being in harmony and peace. We experience ourselves as centered. We feel ourselves at the mid-point of the scale. We have the inner calm to listen and focus. We have self-confidence. We can have a standpoint due to being balanced and centered. The human "I" is strongly involved in this sense.

When we are born, we struggle to achieve balance, especially when we practice standing upright and walking in the gravitational field of the earth. The human figure in its uprightness is the outer expression of our "I". This experience of balance between gravity and levity in our human posture will later become an inner soul balance that makes possible that we hear the inner being of the other person sound through their words.

When this experience of physical balance is fostered in class with various rhythmic activities, by walking on a balance beam, by doing balancing exercises with beanbags, by being perhaps a stork standing on one leg, and so on, then the outer need for balance and harmony will become an inner need for the child, and he will seek to order his life and activities accordingly. Form drawing, especially mirroring exercises, can be helpful in developing this sense. Speech, the art through which the "I" speaks, is excellent to bring balance and help a child feel centered.

Both the sense of movement and the sense of balance under-lie the arithmetic work that the teacher brings in the lower grades. If children struggle to get a relationship to arithmetic, to follow arithmetic problems in the lower grades, they should not get more problems, more intellectual work; rather, the teacher should exercise the senses of movement and balance through activities.

These four will or body senses will be the foundation upon which the higher senses build. We see the importance of developing them in healthy ways.

The four middle senses

The middle senses have a strong feeling component; they are heavily involved with sympathies and antipathies. These senses are caught up in the personal sphere, in wishes, needs and desires, in personal likes and dislikes. The preferences of each person make themselves known in these senses. These four are, therefore, highly affected by the subjective.

The sense of smell connects us with air. We are attracted or repulsed by smells. We surround ourselves with aromas that we cherish, and we have a strong resistance to smells we do not care for. We are pulled out into our environment by the invigorating smells in nature–the fragrant trees and plants, the smell of moist air or a stormy sea. However, we may feel an aversion to the exhaust fumes from buses and trucks on city streets.

The teacher needs to be conscious of the air in the classroom. Fresh air enlivens and wakes up the children, while old socks and T-shirts, a rotting bunch of flowers, or watercolor paints in the jars for several weeks create classroom odors that can give headaches!

We cannot turn off our sense of smell, but we can get used to the smells in the classroom after we are in it for a while. However, everyone appreciates fresh air. It helps the students be present and focused, and it has a positive effect on the sense of life.

The sense of taste connects us with the outside world. For what do we have a taste? Do we like salty, sweet, sour, bitter? Our personal preference for certain tastes may make us choose the same few things on the menu in a restaurant. What is true for the taste of foods also applies to drinks. We use this sense also to judge other things, like style of dress, the beauty of arts, crafts, and furnishings, and so on. In taste works alchemy, giving us an understanding of substances.

For the teacher the question is: How clean, orderly, and beautiful is my classroom? Is the lighting appropriate, the color on the walls tasteful? How do I decorate it to be inviting for the level of my class?

The sense of sight, connected with the eye, is an all-encompassing sense. With the sense of sight the inner soul emerges. We experience light and color. This sense affects our whole being, even our approach to life. Visiting or living in areas where we can only enjoy a few hours of daylight in winter can become for some people very depressing. We become aware in such northern areas of the world how much we need the light.

The sense of sight can be attended to with good lighting conditions and an artistic, color-rich environment. This sense can be refined and enlivened through the art of painting. It is then sensitized to the many different shades of color, the delicate hues, and the great variety of colors in the natural kingdoms about us. All of nature speaks much more to us, even as adults, when, through painting, we notice and appreciate its colors and nuances more vividly. We can observe the play of light and the display of delicate colors in a rainbow, sunrises, and sunsets. This play of color is immensely enriching for the soul. When souls breathe color, they feel well.

Rudolf Steiner gave indications for specific colors to be used in painting the walls of each classroom.

Caring for the senses is the mission of the arts.

The sense of warmth makes us aware of the warmth of our own and other bodies. Human beings need warmth. We are sensitive to temperature, to outer warmth and cold, as well as to soul warmth. How we experience life has much to do with how we are received into this life. To feel wanted is essential for the health of the child. How were we received into this world by our parents? How much love and warmth, how much joy was around us? All this the child perceives, even before birth.

In the classroom every child needs to feel included. Is every child treated in the same supportive way? Is the mood heartwarm? If the teacher enjoys what she is doing, the children will feel surrounded by warmth. What a feeling of well-being!

These middle senses bring us into close contact with our natural and human environment. We take the world into ourselves when we smell it, taste it, feel it. The middle senses call forth our personal reactions. We can be overly sensitive to the warmth or the cold approaching us from our social environment.

The four upper senses

As we mentioned before, the upper senses make human social life possible. With these four knowledge senses we get to know the other human being. By listening to the speech of the other person, we can perceive the thoughts and individuality of the one who speaks. The whole human being communicates with us. These four senses give us the possibility of encountering the true being of the other, her soul and her individual spirit.

Social life *is* communication. To be social we need a certain measure of selflessness. So, we can also call these upper senses the selfless senses. They need to have a certain amount of selflessness to create a healthy social life.

The sense of hearing is strongly connected with the senses of balance and movement. Hearing and balance share the same sense organ as physical location. This is, I think, for a good reason. The child needs inner calm to listen and focus, needs balance in the soul realm, before the quality of speech, the emphasis on words, the many nuances of sounds can be deciphered. He has to learn to hear them.

Listening, we grow out into the world. We must forget ourselves to do so. Listening requires will effort; it requires focus, which means the "I" is actively present. Are we too preoccupied with ourselves to hear the other individual? Hearing is a question of interest and motivation. It is also clear that for listening a certain amount of selflessness is necessary. Perhaps this is the reason why listening is a challenge in our present time.

Children love to hear stories. They journey with the teacher to faraway places. They leave the classroom, move out, and experience the dense forest, the magnificent palace, the cave beneath the earth. They see the gnomes, the fairies, the elves. Hearing stories, the children's listening capacity increases. With storytelling, the teacher can develop this capacity, especially when the story lives in the room, when she uses many descriptive images, and speaks slowly enough, with a voice coming from the heart, not from the head.

The sense of speech enables us to find meaning in what we hear spoken. Can the child pay attention to spoken words, decipher gestures, understand pauses, and follow the flow of a sentence? Is the child "in tune" with the spoken word? Can the child hear the different sounds, discern the new words in a story, and integrate them when retelling? Do gestures, forms, and movements speak to the child? The sense of speech gives us the ability to hear the words spoken by the other, including their sound and structure.

The child listens to the teacher speak for many years. Therefore, the teacher needs to be conscious of her speech and should embrace extensive speech work. Her speech should be well-formed, heart-warm, clear, slow enough, not squeaky and high, so that the child can inwardly picture while the teacher speaks. Speaking at a speed that enables the other to receive and understand what is said is particularly important in our time when "fast-speak" is the dominant habit—as fast as possible. With that kind of speech, who can really think along, let alone have the time to form images?

The spoken word is very much being degraded in our time. Electronic media, having gained access into every corner of life, demand our attention. Teenagers and adults often center their activities on their use. For the teacher it can be a struggle to keep them out of the classroom. Through them the child hears electronic words that transmit no life, no soul, no "I" presence, and no ethical, moral quality rays out to the child as it does from the spoken word. Words without soul cannot nourish the growing child. Healing forces can stream to the child only through the human, non-electronic word. Human language carries a quality of soul and spirit to the child and becomes a leaven for him. The individual reveals himself in his speech. Rudolf Steiner points out that an actual being presides over a language, called the genius of the language. It is an archangelic being who can send its forces through human speech, especially when this speech contains the life element of rhythm, rhyme, and melody.

The sense of thought enables us to perceive the thoughts of others, not our own. We perceive our own thoughts directly; we do not need a special sense to do that. We are the ones thinking our thoughts; they are clear to us. The thoughts of the other person are revealed in their speaking, although thoughts can also be communicated in many other ways: through works of art, through movement and gestures, through facial expressions. Mimes are experts in relating thoughts through other ways than speech.

To take in the thoughts of another, we have to make room for them by silencing our own thoughts. We can then experience that perceiving the thoughts and concepts of another is an intuitive capacity. Our understanding is intuitive. Something of a purely soul-spiritual nature is perceived by us. The question then arises: Is it possible to raise this sense to the level that we can perceive the divine creative thoughts in nature and in the universe?

The sense of thought is a metamorphosis of the sense of life. They share the same organ; it is the totality of our life organization that perceives thoughts.

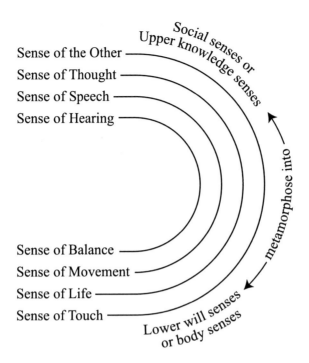

Sense of the Other
Sense of Thought
Sense of Speech
Sense of Hearing

Sense of Balance
Sense of Movement
Sense of Life
Sense of Touch

Upper knowledge senses or Social senses

metamorphose into

Lower will senses or body senses

Metamorphosis of the lower will senses
into the knowledge –social senses.

As teacher we need to see if the child follows the thoughts expressed in spoken language. Can the student decipher meaning? Can he retain meaning spanning several sentences?

Can he follow and understand the teacher's presentation? Are there frequent misunderstandings? Is the child too restless to pick up the inner meaning? Too distracted? Too tired?

The sense of thought unites us with other human beings. We need this social sense to perceive and understand the other person. Thinking is an activity full of life and imagination. The nineteenth-century German poet, Friedrich Schiller, experienced thoughts and words in a living way: "Thought is my boundless realm, and my winged instrument is the word!"[69] Today we generally perceive thoughts after they have been formed, that is, when they are finished, when they have lost their quality of life, when they find expression.

The sense of the other, sometimes called the sense of the ego, means having a sense of the other's ego. Through the working of this sense, we can obtain at least an inkling of the other's true being, his or her true essence. The organ for this sense of the other is the whole body. This sense is a metamorphosis of the sense of touch.

When we turn to the child, we can ask ourselves: How does the child connect with other human beings? Is there trust? Can he form a relationship with teachers, with classmates? Does he shy away, is there fear? We can detect fairly easily with this sense if something is amiss. Does the student respect others, respect what belongs to them, or is there a lack of perception of the other? When reading a book, can he identify with the protagonist?

To develop this "I" sense, the teacher can work with her Main Lesson and balance its four parts. Does it have a good breathing, is there rhythm? Is there a balance between listening and doing? On the soul level, the teacher can work with speech and drama. Careful attention can also be given to the yearly block rotation. Some subjects bring the ego in, and some lead the ego out into the world. In other words, does the Main Lesson block emphasize in-breathing or out-breathing. Is it a math block or a geography block?[70]

Through the twelve senses we direct the child's attention to the forms, colors, gestures, moods, expressions of nature and its seasonal transformation. Through the sense of the other, the child can apprehend the eternal spiritual nature of another human being, and experience the thought content of the other, the speech of the other. Only with a healthy development of the upper or knowledge senses may a healthy social life be established. This can come out of the free recognition of the sacredness of the other individual.

In our time and culture the upper senses are ignored. In the lecture, "The Work of the Angels in Man's Astral Body."[71] Steiner discusses the importance of a healthy social future, in which humanity awakens to a threefold truth that will re-sound through human souls like cosmic music:

• Complete freedom of religion for the soul of every human being will be respected.

• The sacred divinity in each human being will become apparent in every real human encounter.

• Strengthened thinking will be able to cross a threshold to penetrate into spiritual reality.

Becoming conscious of the spiritual essence in humans will have as its consequence that no one will find peace or happiness in the future if others beside him are suffering. Human brotherhood will be the goal.

In the light of these thoughts, has the teacher sensitized her soul to what lives in the individual students, perhaps still in a hidden way? Is it possible for her to develop a sense of the divine essence?

It is crucial for social health that we begin to have real encounters in which we experience the true being of the other.

All sense perception is the foundation for our discerning activity, our judgment. We perceive the world through our differentiated senses. Our "I" synthesizes the information and we can form judgments, make decisions, and discern a situation. When we experience in ourselves or in others an inability to make decisions or form clear judgments, we can see in this inability the consequence of undifferentiated sense-perception in childhood. Judging is a living process. Our senses give us half the truth, the other half must be added by us, by finding the proper concept through our thinking activity. We bring our sense-perceptions together in a healthy judging ability.

Forming a relation with the body

Rudolf Steiner speaks about childhood diseases and points out that they may have their beginning in a lack of healthy breathing (taken in the broadest sense) and in the lack of a healthy integration of soul-spirit with life-body, which is, of course, also a breathing process (We breathe our soul-spirit in and breathe it out again.) Going back to the traditional childhood diseases accompanied by fever, we can sense in them the work of the child's ego making an ultimate effort through the increase of warmth in the body to bring about a healthier relationship between the individuality and his biology.

What Rudolf Steiner brought early on in the twentieth century is recognized today by some scientists. K. Golenhofen, for one, in his book, *Physiology Today*,[72] gives an example regarding mental arithmetic, a "heady," cognitive activity. He points out that this activity is always connected with the blood-flow through the muscle system, the skin, the heart function, as well as other bodily functions. He shows that mental arithmetic increases the blood-flow through the muscle system 300% when compared to a condition of rest, and the pulse frequency increases up to 120 heart beats per minute. These numbers might not mean much to us as such, but when we hear that these values are equal to those of heavy physical work, it is immediately clear to us that these seemingly "heady" processes affect the whole body.

As teachers we must be aware of this interconnectedness. Only then can we understand the nervous reaction and unrest some children display when the teacher proceeds perhaps too long with this mental activity. When that occurs, children are drawn to the opposite pole; they need to get into their limbs and run around. We understand from this that the method of instruction not only has an effect on the learning of the child but is physiologically relevant to his health. Steiner continually points to the effect of learning on the whole child and neurobiology now confirms his findings.

Joachim Bauer, physician and professor, explains this effect from his neurobiological research:

> Teaching is interaction and where humans interact...
> the brain transforms interaction into biological signals, that is, relationships work into the biology, into the ability to learn. The brain changes psychology into biology and neurobiological activity works into psy-

chology–into experience and behavior. The biological consequences of interactive relationships do not only affect the here and now in any given situation, but they leave behind...a biological script with long-term effects.[73]

He confirms the long-term effects that Steiner pointed out long ago, showing how life is a whole and what happens in childhood has an effect on the health or illness later in life. Bauer further states:

All school activities are embedded in interactive and dialogue-based activities. Where human interaction is at play, it is also always about neurobiology...Everything that humans experience in relationships is changed by the brain into biological signals; it works on and affects our biology, the achievement capacity of our body, and influences our behavior. This in turn works back onto our relationships.[74] [translated by author].

And in addition, recent neurobiological studies show that the essential prerequisites for the biological functional efficiency of our motivation systems are interest, social recognition, and personal appreciation extended from one person to another. According to Bauer:

As mentioned previously, the brain changes psychological impressions into biological signals. To express it casually, the brain makes psychology out of biology. Studies could show that social exclusion or isolation inactivate certain genes in our motivational systems. The other way around, we could say that the mere expectation of recognition and appreciation shows massive activation of these systems.[75]

Only when the caregiver personally shows interest in the child does the feeling arise in the child that he is important, that life has meaning. If this is absent, then we see the signs that we know from a great many young people. As Bauer says:

The body looks for alternative stimuli that can activate and, rather, corrupt the motivational systems of the brain to get to the essential neurotransmitters. Alternative stimuli of this kind have a dangerous disadvantage, they can destroy human life: addictive drugs, computer gaming addiction, Internet, the virtual world. Computer games disconnect from the real world and compromise their actual developmental possibilities.[76]

Bauer's insights continue to confirm what Rudolf Steiner pointed out already in the first third of the twentieth century, namely that the entire body is affected by what we think, feel, and do.

What about our typical childhood diseases?

In our time, we do not see only a quantitative but also a qualitative change in the health situation of our children and young people. In general we can say, we see less of what we called the typical childhood diseases, like measles, mumps, chicken pox, and so on, although every now and then one or the other flares up again. These illnesses usually are accompanied by a fever, as I said, in the increase of the temperature, the "I" of the child becomes active and makes strong efforts to connect with the physical body via the warmth element. In place of these childhood diseases we now see rather many "unspecific ailments" (an expression coined by Hurrelmann, 1997), such as concentration and attention deficits, psychosomatic illnesses like headaches, stomachaches, digestive problems, sleep and eating disorders, even light sensitivity, hyperkinesias, behavior problems affecting social situations, learning problems, fear and stress-related problems, depression, aggression, auditory and visual and speech disturbances, Asperger and autism-related challenges–the list goes on and on, and I do not want to add teacher depression to this list, therefore, I will stop here! As teachers you are dealing with a number of these symptoms and challenges in your students every day.

Observing in classrooms and speaking with teachers, I have felt on the whole that some common sense and balance needs to be reestablished in the soul of the teacher. There is too much focus on what is wrong with individual students. I noticed at times a certain feeling of helplessness taking over a teacher. There seemed to be a leaden weight on a teacher's shoulders. I would therefore like to challenge the teacher to look more carefully at these unspecific ailments mentioned, and you may notice that the most dominant factor in them is the deficit in the child's relation to his own body; a healthy connection is lacking. When we can recognize a common denominator in these various ailments, then, perhaps, we can find some ground under our feet again. Then perhaps, we can change our focus from seeing the glass half empty to seeing it half full.

As teachers we must be conscious to balance our focus. We must practice consciously to develop loving attention to all that is positive in each child. Each child brings many abilities, also new qualities much needed in our time, often referred to as a strong will component. When we find an inner balance, then we as teachers can be more optimistic, joyful, and then gratitude will fill the classroom. This is a call to inner activity of the teacher! Your additional inner effort to connect with the spiritual, individual core of the child will be a significant strengthening of your relationship with the student. This effort will bring you closer to the children, and from resiliency research we know that the immune system is strengthened most of all by good, positive, supportive relationships.

Integrating rhythm into teaching

We have a healer inside us: the rhythmic system. It is our very own doctor. Health is bound to a well-flowing, rhythmic order of the life functions and processes. Disturbances in this order cause illness.[77] Every organ lives in a field of tension of anabolism and catabolism, regenerating and tiring, sleeping and waking, healing and becoming ill. Rhythm comes about as a need to mediate between these polarities. Health is not something that *exists* but something that must be established every moment anew through the mediation of our rhythmic system. This system establishes harmony and balance in our breathing, and between the world and the self. Rhythm supports children's learning and strengthens their life-forces. Their development needs a rhythmic flow in time and repetition of familiar learning in many different ways to establish inner security, confidence, and trust. A rhythmic flow in what we do with the children every day helps them with their orientation in space and time. In addition, it creates a stable environment and supports the development of a healthy memory. The rhythmic system is indeed our healer inside.

As Waldorf teachers we consciously integrate rhythm into all of our teaching through an artistic element, through in -breathing and out-breathing in our lessons, and by working with the elements of joyful lightness or sadness. In addition, we make sure that there is a balance in our lessons between listening and doing. We consider the rhythm in our daily and weekly schedules, and in our yearly block-rotation. It is quite a challenge in an established school to create a healthy schedule for the whole school. With the yearly block-rotation it is especially important to be aware of the in- and out-breathing quality, so that we follow a block of arithmetic with, for example, a block of geography. We enable the children to connect with their self in the inner activity of thinking (mathematics) and then move out again into the world (geography).

In addition to the yearly rhythm, each block and subject contains elements both of in-breathing and out-breathing. Of these we must be aware in our daily teaching. There the teacher needs to alternate between the in-breathing, reflective element and the active, hands-on, practical activities. She needs to harmonize these through a feeling heart, for it is feeling that is connected with the rhythmic system. The block-rotation designed by each class teacher will ideally consist of a four-week time span in the lower grades (grades 1 and 2). This time-span supports and strengthens the etheric-life and healing forces of the child, because the four-week rhythm is the rhythm of the etheric body. In the weekly schedule how the specialty classes are arranged, (for instance, how eurythmy is placed in connection with physical education, or foreign languages in connection with these two) has an effect on the feeling life and is the rhythm of the astral body. Children feel subconsciously how this scheduling affects their well-being. The daily schedule affects the ego, which is embedded in the twenty-four-hour rhythm of sleeping and waking. Here, the actual rhythm in our daily Main Lesson is experienced. The Main Lesson is really an artistic creation, addressing the whole child in thinking, feeling, and willing, helping the child to incarnate at the beginning of Main Lesson and to excarnate at the end of Main Lesson.

Main Lesson

Rhythmic activity = Incarnating activity

8:30–9:00 rhythmic part (circle time) addresses: **feeling** (willing)

9:00–9:30 review of work and new aspects of the work addresses: **thinking**/memory/head

9:30–10:00 Main Lesson book work addresses: **will** activity/writing/artistic work

10:00–10:30 Story time (also review/retell the story) addresses: **inner** picture-**thinking, feeling,** and **willing**

Story element = Excarnating activity followed by recess

Looking at the chart above, we can experience the rhythm and flow of the Main Lesson. It becomes clear that Steiner thought through every aspect so that by the end of the lesson the whole child has been addressed. It is crucial to notice this, for when this or that teacher thinks, "Oh, why don't I just change that and lengthen movement to 45 minutes or even an hour, then skip the writing part in the Main Lesson and do it later in a practice period. That will give me more time for other things in the Main Lesson." Yet, Main Lesson is a completely artistic creation in itself. If we take away the balance that today's students especially need, then we fail to address the whole child in our Main Lesson. Balance is fundamental when we speak of a healing education. Please note that the Main Lesson starts with an incarnating activity and ends with an excarnating activity. The uniqueness of this education shows itself in every detail.

Block preparation: teaching through pictures

Rudolf Steiner emphasized the importance of including the feeling life in all learning. This understanding is recognized today in neurobiology. The remark by Manfred Spitzer, prominent psychologist at the University of Ulm, Germany, underlines this insight: "The role of emotions in learning can hardly be overestimated."[78]

Steiner takes the assertion further by emphasizing that if we teach too intellectually, if we focus on the intellect by explaining things to the child instead of giving pictures, descriptions, and characterizations, then the breathing process of the child is affected. We might even lay the groundwork of a tendency toward asthma. In the US, one out of ten children struggles with asthma. (American Academy of Allergy, Asthma and Immunology, 2011). Might this be connected with an overly-intellectual education?

Overemphasizing the intellect can bring other illnesses to the fore. Physician and author Heinz Herbert Schoeffler writes of the intellectual stress many children experience: "It has been known for a long time that not only psychological stress but actually continuous intellectual stress is responsible for the manifestation of diabetes."[79]

On the other side, Steiner points out that a child taught with pictures and images will be a person still fresh and active up into his or her late age. When teaching is directed only to understanding and intellect, then the individual will age early and be susceptible to conditions that bring illness.[80] It is a question of working either with or against the life forces in the child.

We can transform logical, cognitive activity into artistic expression. We can ask, "How do I prepare the material for each block artistically, to retain life and imagination? How do I get a good flow, so that the block has a beginning, a middle, and an end?" We should not just stop when three or four weeks are over. How can I be prepared well enough so that I am not bound to every word of my preparation but can bring what is needed on that day, for these children, with the right pictures, considering the moment, the here and the now. It might be a help to take the following steps into consideration:

First step: For every block read what Steiner originally said about it. You need leading ideas: What is essential for this block? What does this block address in the child? How should I approach the block. What are the key ideas? Read up on your block in Karl Stockmeyer's book, *Rudolf Steiner's Curriculum for Waldorf Schools*. Also look to *The Tasks and Content of the Steiner-Waldorf Curriculum* by Kevin Avison and Martin Rawson.

Second step: When you have a picture of the block, gather materials concerning the subject to be presented. Research the topic. You need a clear overview, so that you feel at ease with the subject, at least as far as you will take it in a particular year. Get a feeling of what speaks to you, what excites you about this block. What other subjects might you weave in with it? Now plan your block. (preparation on the physical level/layout)

Third step: Inwardly shape the presentation. Ask yourself, where do I feel a personal relationship, a connection? Where is my interest? How and where do I want to start it, what do I want to highlight, where and how do I want to end? How will it fit into the flow of my block. How far do I want to get in the block, during each week, on any particular day? (preparation on the etheric level/time element)

Fourth step: Inwardly picture your entire presentation. Have it before you in your mind's eye. Remember that the world needs to speak to the child through you, the teacher. Let the child experience your relationship to the world, your interest in it. Bring details with loving attention: how the streets looked, the buildings, what the people wore, what sandals, hats and so on, what the weather was like; in other words, descriptive details. These will assist the children in forming their inner pictures well and precisely. It will also establish a stronger feeling relationship. (preparation on the astral level/ feelings, relationships, pictures)

Fifth step: On the "I"-level you can now integrate everything to get an overview within the time frame. Only now is the teacher ready to give the presentation to the class, with total presence of mind, giving her full attention. Now we realize that the beginning (our first and second steps), our thorough preparation, gives us the ease and the freedom that ideas, and inspirations will come in the moment. The "I"-level is also present in the artistic method that the teacher chooses. She can look at each child and realize that each has his own path, his own genius, and that my way may not be the way every child can understand it. Then a question lives in the teacher: How do I bring the material so that it becomes accessible to each child? Here it is important that I do not cling to the details of my preparation, I am able to let them go. A conscious forgetting is possible, so that I am open for inspirations, intuitions, ideas that come in the act of creating. That is the artistic method. (Engagement of the "I")

To go through these helpful steps takes time. The presentation needs to be contemplated thoroughly and pictured, for only then will you be comfortable and at ease enough in the classroom to meet where the children are on a particular day and change your presentation should you need to.

When a detailed picture lives in you, then you can describe and characterize the events from different sides; you can compare and contrast. Then life, movement, and artistry enter into your presentation, and this builds character. And yes, this takes effort and preparation. When you can present out of the picture you have before you, then you also meet the needs of today's overloaded children. You will live so strongly in the events you are describing that you will draw the students into the situations that will arise before them. All of us as teachers have experienced how fabulous it feels and what life there can be in the classroom, what infectious atmosphere, when we succeed in this. Of course, there are times when we do not succeed and we know how this feels, too!

Steiner gives us this insight: Only when the teacher has connected with the subject and really lives in it can she engage the interest of the children sufficiently. Only when the teacher is engaged and interested in what she presents does the child come inwardly into movement. He also makes it clear that in the future the teacher will have to make a far greater effort to draw the children into the presentation.[81] The future Rudolf Steiner speaks about is now.

Is it possible for the teacher to connect with the material as intimately and intensively as needed to draw today's children sufficiently into the lesson when the teacher is tied closely to her music stand holding her notes? That is the question. Can the teacher really regroup the material in her mind when needed? Can the presentation become a living, artistic process? Can the teacher add or change in the moment to emphasize, elaborate, or sense what the class needs? The teacher must live in the creative moment with the necessary enthusiasm and interest. Otherwise, all is "precooked," so to speak. Then, there is too little meat in the presentation, too little of the creative act in it. The "imponderables" (Steiner) then are not as strongly at work as they should be. (I am not talking here about having a few dates or names written down). Preparing thoroughly is not only beneficial for the students right down into their physical health, but it also works back on the teacher. Such strong identification with the subject invigorates the etheric life forces, which in turn strengthens the immune system. It is the opposite of "multi-tasking," which is one of the worst things for our etheric body. It gets pulled into too many directions. "Because of the tenuous interest... the etheric body is gradually weakened."[82]

In the first lecture of the *Study of Man*, Steiner speaks of the task of the teacher as bringing "the soul-spirit into harmony with the life-body." The teacher has the task to make sure that the individuality of the child coming from spiritual worlds and trying to incarnate into a physical body connects with it in a healthy way. The physical body supplied by the hereditary stream needs to become the child's earthly home, the earthly tool that makes it possible to manifest his deeds in the world. What a very different task for the teacher, an inspiring task. How can we accomplish such a task? (See: The teacher's main task, p. 67).

Steiner points to the breathing process, indicating that the two different entities can be harmonized by a third system: the rhythmic system. The polarity of heavenly and earthly human being must be harmonized. When the soul-spiritual entity cannot take hold of the body well enough, then we see a child not in her limbs, not grounded enough (see page 69).

In one of my classes a child struggled from first grade on to walk on her whole foot. She only walked on tiptoes. The rhythmic activities at the beginning of Main Lesson, the work in the garden, the planting of wheat near the end of second grade, and the practical activities in the third grade eventually brought her down to earth with the nine-year change. This is the time when creation stories are told, like the story of Adam and Eve who must leave paradise and make their home on the earth. How amazingly appropriate!

Another way to see that a child is not taking sufficient hold of the body is if he is spacey, oblivious to what is happening around him, does not easily pay attention and listens only briefly and intermittently, is often in his own world.

On the other hand, if the soul is drawn too deeply into the physical body, if the soul-spiritual becomes as if imprisoned in it, the child can be restless, not able to sit still, become irritated, even aggressive. We may see this behavior also if the child is exposed to a lot of media, where the fascination with television or tablet pulls the individual strongly into the physical, material environment, even into the sub-earthly environment of electricity (see page 71).

Seeking the eternal being in the child is illness prevention. The child feels recognized. Rudolf Steiner goes further to show us how our efforts with the children work not only into this incarnation, but into the following. It is good to bring to our consciousness that the astral body (our feelings and emotions) tends toward being an egoist here on earth, but if we succeed in connecting the child well with the surrounding world, by awakening his interest in it and love for it, then in the following life this will mean the formation of a healthy astral body. If we can awaken compassion and social consideration for others in the student, the consequence in the following life will be a healthy soul life.

How do we individualize our teaching?

Within the last years the matter of individualizing instruction has become a question for teachers. Parents want their child to receive one-on-one time. Therefore, a teacher may wonder: Am I individualizing enough? I have seen this approach go overboard on numerous occasions; for instance, in the foreign language classes. The teacher keeps calling on individual children, even as the class is not only getting restless but literally falling apart. Rather than pulling the class together by engaging all children together in an activity, the one-on-one is continued far too long. The breathing between the whole class and the individual child has to be handled well by the teacher. We must, of course, individualize, just not over-individualize. A good rule of thumb is usually: the whole class speaks together (in recitation), then three or four children speak individually, then the whole class together again, then three or four children individually. This rhythm works well most of the time. This is a general suggestion. Classes differ, as teachers know. When a class is restless, you might reduce the individual interaction to one or two children, or you might even decide that today is a day for drawing, writing, or reading, depending on the class level.

We can ask ourselves as teachers, "What does *individualizing* really mean?"

It was only recently that I discovered Steiner addresses this issue, too. He puts into perspective what individualization actually is and what it is not:

> What we call individualizing happens by itself if the teacher is really in touch with the children who are before him, and if she is also actively connected with the world. Then what she brings and how she brings it, will be so interesting that the children will listen, and then they are engaged in actively individualizing themselves! If they individualize themselves, it is

done actively, they are inwardly active. Then you do not need to occupy yourself with each individual student constantly, for when you do, you individualize passively.[83]

Individualizing passively means that the teacher is doing the individualizing, not the child. The teacher is calling on individual children; they themselves are not picking and choosing what fits them; they are not inwardly self-engaged in the process. What should happen, according to Steiner, is that the students would be so interested that they would listen closely and then take from the presentation what they individually need. That is what Steiner calls "active" individualization. It is of far greater benefit to the students, because the higher Self knows itself, and it knows its direction in life and what it needs. When teachers leave it up to the child's "I" to take what it needs, then we leave the child free to individualize himself.

We see here that Steiner speaks of active and passive individualization. We need to keep in mind that transformation, maturation, and inner development occur through active inner engagement by the student. This is true as well for adults.

Focusing on the young child, we can ask: Where do we see that the child individualizes actively? Or put another way, where do we see the child's higher Self becoming active in guiding the child? With the young child we see it in the activity of free play. When we encourage free play at home or in a Waldorf kindergarten, our job as adults should be to make sure that we supply the age-appropriate stimulating environment. Only then do we create the preconditions for making active individualization possible for each child at that age. What happens in play is accomplished through the activity of the child himself, and that is what Steiner calls to our attention. No adult should interfere, instruct, or give directives. We leave the child to his own resources. What do we notice when we observe the child? The child is busily engaged, perhaps hangs a sheet, it falls down. He picks it up again, tries again, it falls down again. He looks around, finds clothes pins, clips it up, it stays. The child tries out how his own actions work on the objects in his environment.

Peek-a-boo, I see you!

His own creative will is activated. Steiner points to something important here, namely, the child is "learning from life itself." Life educates the child. That is why it is necessary not to interfere with intellectual, thought-out directives. Something higher than the intellect can approach the child in his activities, something beyond the mere persona. It is the higher Self that works on the child here. The more play leads to an experience of life, the better it is for the child.[84]

Another activity is the pedagogical story (see page 109). Here we can observe how the Self of the child selects from the story what he needs for his own progress, for his own biography.

Intellect does not build character; it does not bring us inner maturity, inner moral development. Character is built when children (and all of us, for that matter) are interested, when they identify, when they love. Under those circumstances the character configuration of the child can find its path quickly. (As with young adults falling in love, change can almost come overnight.)

Of course, the story and later the history element also work strongly in this individualizing process, on character building, on supplying a moral foundation. This element encompasses to a large extent that part of the Waldorf curriculum that we designate as "know thyself," in which we can see destiny and karma working, while on the other hand, geography and the sciences lead the student to "interest in the world."

I want to add here a captivating story that goes into the destiny question and might even be interesting for students in the high school. Given the right situation, it can stimulate much thought and good conversation. (It is not for the very young child, even for a second grade one would have to work with it differently.)

"A native Indian boy was climbing high up in the mountains, when suddenly he spied an eagle's egg. He picked it up carefully and decided to take it down into the valley where he lived. There he laid it into a chicken coop for a hen to sit on and hatch. And so it happened. The little eaglet grew up with the young chicks in a yard. It scratched in the sand, picked the seeds, and every now and then it spread its wings and flew to the lower branches of close-by trees. One day the young eaglet looked up into the sky, and there he saw the most magnificent bird he had ever seen, circling high up in the sun light. He could not take his eyes off that bird. "What kind of glorious bird is this so high up that he is almost touching the sun?" it asked the chick next to him. "That is a Golden Eagle, the king of the air," was the reply. "But don't look up. You and I, we are chickens, we will never soar to such heights." The young eagle followed that advice. He became old and gray and finally died, believing he was a chicken."[85]

Dear teachers, I ask you, who wants to be a chicken when in reality he is an eagle? It is essential that we, the teachers, discover the eagle in our students and give them the confidence to explore the many different possibilities that their individual destinies have in store for them. We want to make sure that they may gradually find the eagle in themselves, for how many people are happy with being a chicken because they do not recognize the eagle inside!

Assisting with developmental steps

At times it is good to refresh the mind by thinking in a different way, in a reverse way, about something that we have accepted as "being like that." As Waldorf teachers we may assume that the seven-year developmental steps are something all children go through naturally. When we look at our time, though, and the challenges children bring teachers, we need to change this perspective. We cannot assume anymore that these steps Rudolf Steiner indicated for child development will happen in a natural way. It is not a given anymore that children go through the seven-year steps naturally on their own. Children can miss important steps, or go through them in a disharmonious way.

Therefore, it is now the task of the Waldorf teacher to assist the child to take hold of the developmental tasks that each of the seven-year period poses. These steps address questions to the teacher: What is essential for these seven years, and how do I as teacher guide the child towards a proper unfolding of these developmental steps? Waldorf teachers must strive as much as possible to let the children work out of the impulses designated for the specific seven-year period that they enter, and not rush ahead because the intellect of the child wants to push ahead. For when the designated time for a certain step in development has passed, the development may be missed. In our time much thought and work are needed to establish a healthy physical body between birth and the age of seven, a healthy life body (ages 7-14), and a healthy astral-feeling-body (ages 12-18). For example, if the astral is freed too early and addressed before the etheric body is fully developed, then healthy development may be stunted, with consequences for life.

From birth to seven years of age, the child needs to work out of the forces that he brought with him from the spiritual world. These are the forces of imitation. The physical body learns through imitation, through identifying with the adults in the environment. As Steiner says, "What is to an adult a separate visual perception, the child experiences in the whole body;

and without any forethought a child's will impulses take the shape of reflexes. A child's whole body responds reflexively to every impression in the environment."[86]

Neurobiology confirms this assertion. Albert Bandura, professor emeritus at Stanford University, well known for his learning theory, speaks of "learning from the model." In the 1990s a neuro-biological center in the brain was discovered that works "automatically, without conscious thought" and its "sole purpose is to simulate the observed behavior of other people in the brain of the observer, to copy in a silent way the actions, feelings, moods; everything that others do, is imitated in the brain of the observer as in a mirror." The nerve cells specializing in this activity are named, "mirror neurons." The imitation Rudolf Steiner speaks about is called "participatory-acting."[87] Joachim Bauer, physician and professor of psychosomatics, adds therefore "the relationships to adults play a decisive role."[88]

All activity of soul and spirit in the human being has physical correlates in the child. The "mirror neurons" are one of the physical correlates, so that the soul spiritual forces the child brings with him from the spiritual world can act in the child. Steiner guides us to begin with observation:

> Let us study the human being as he appears to us today, beginning with the child up to the change of teeth. We see quite clearly that his physical development runs parallel with his development of soul and spirit. Everything that manifests as soul and spirit has its exact counterpart in the physical – both appear together; both develop out of the child together.[89]

Yet he wants us to realize that there is much involved that goes beyond observation.

> We do not only have those soul qualities within us that had their beginning at birth or at conception, but we bear within us pre-earthly qualities of soul, indeed, we bear within us the results of past earthly lives. All this lives and works and weaves within us…We must therefore understand how the super-sensible works

into the earthly life...It works only in a hidden way into the bodily nature, and one does not understand the body if one has no understanding of the spiritual forces active within it.[90]

We must understand the invisible if the visible is to make sense.

Creating pedagogical stories

Rudolf Steiner incorporated pedagogical stories as a unique element of Waldorf education. These brief stories, created by the teacher in grades one through three, hold a mirror up to behaviors occurring in the classroom. How should these behaviors be addressed by the teacher? The pedagogical stories speak to the children by objectifying a particular situation. The teacher creates a brief story illustrating the child's behavior through, for example, the activities of an animal, making it easier for the child to listen and identify with the activities and their outcome than a direct reprimand might accomplish. Objectifying the behavior means making up a story so the child can experience his behavior mirrored in the animal world.

With the young child everything comes from outside. The behavior is dressed into story pictures. Through these stories the teacher addresses the higher Self of the child directly. This higher Self or "I" is the transforming, form-giving, integrating agent in the human being. These brief stories should not replace the fairy tale, legend, or other main story told at the end of Main Lesson. The pedagogical stories are of a different nature and purpose than the main stories. They are best placed at or toward the beginning of Main Lesson to set a mood and create room for change. Creating these little stories is made easier for the teacher when she has three steps in mind:

1. What animal family would be good as an image to elucidate this particular behavior?

A. Clever foxes that love to trick others?

B. Fast little mice that run all over, not listening?

C. Squawking geese that make a dreadful noise?

2. Create a similar behavioral situation with the animal character as occurred in the classroom.

A. One little fox takes things from others and hides them away.

B. A fast little mouse running all over not listening to what mama and papa mouse had asked.

C. A squawking goose making so much noise when warned to be quiet that the fox has an easy target, and so on.

3. Place consequences at the end of the story. Children cannot yet understand nor predict consequences in the early grades.

A. The others are upset at the little fox and exclude him from their fun and games.

B. The little mouse is trapped because he did not hear his parents warn all little mice not to go near the traps.

C. The fox comes along and hunts the goose, and either snaps off the tail feathers and the goose escapes, or the fox has a good supper.

The teacher has to gauge how strong the consequences need to be in a particular case and class. Some stories should be more on the gentle side (depending on the grade). However, if the problems persist, a story with sterner consequences might be appropriate. In the US, I have observed that teachers tend to err on the side of being too gentle so that the consequence is not perceived and therefore the effect of the story is negligible.

As a class teacher I was amazed at the healing power of these self-created stories. The children loved them. When greeting them in the morning I was regularly asked: "Do you have a story for us?" This question always referred to the pedagogical story. Since you as teacher create the story for your class, or for a group of children or an individual in the class, something special takes place that Steiner describes as "imponderables" (I have mentioned these before) and begins to weave between teacher and children. Through these daily little stories, a deep bond with the class is established. The higher Self of each child, her true being is addressed in these pedagogical stories. The teacher never explains anything, leaving it to the freedom of each child's "I" to decide what it needs to take from the story. This is a powerful "I"-strengthening activity.

Examples of pedagogical stories

The Seven Little Foxes

There once were seven little foxes, and they loved to play with each other all day long, just like you, dear children. They would jump on top of each other, run from each other and catch one another, bump into each other, nudge each other, even chew on each other's paws or ears, pulling on the fur. This is what animals do. Everything, however, was always done playfully, done gently, for fun. On other occasions they liked to run through the forest to see who would win: over rocks, under branches, through the creek water, up a hill, down the other side. They had what we would call an *obstacle course*, a very particular route. They had to concentrate very hard so that they would not make any mistakes when they followed their path of over and under to see who would be the fastest.

Well, dear children, there was one little fox that just did not like to play this game with the others. So he decided it would be fun to disrupt the game. He ran in between the others and made them go off course, he jumped on them and made them tumble, he tried to catch their tail to slow them down, he even tried to bite them, and because they were running, this often turned out to be much too hard. He had no interest in letting the others enjoy their game because he did not want to participate in it. He only wanted all of them to play what *he* wanted.

This had gone on for some time and the others got very angry because they were always interrupted. One day, Mama and Papa announced that many fox families were getting together and all the little ones were having a race. Oh, how exciting this would be! All little foxes were looking forward to that special day. Our little disturber now said: Oh, how much fun this will be, I will run, too! But Mama and Papa fox now said:

111

Little one, you have always disturbed your brothers and sisters, you have always complained, you were always unhappy and dissatisfied about their game. Now you may not come along. You will stay at home all day. Perhaps you will learn to be a good sport and help instead of ruining the game. The little fox was so very sad and he wished from the bottom of his heart that he had never been so mean as to disrupt their running game over and over again.

The Family of Ducks

There once was a family of ducks living on the side of a lovely lake where many other ducks also stayed. There was Papa duck and Mama duck and six little ducklings. Often they went out on the lake with their father or mother, and they stayed close to them, for they knew that their father and mother loved them and protected them.

The little ducklings loved to play on and on. They loved to peck gently at each other, and chase each other, of course in the water, for ducks cannot run on land very well! In the water, however, they feel quite at home.

One day Papa and Mama ducks called their little ones together and said, "Listen carefully now to what we say! On the other side of the lake there is the home of the sly fox, and he loves to have a good dinner! Do not swim across to the other side of the lake, and certainly do not go on land on the other side. Do not enter the forest that looks so lovely over there! Have you all listened? Otherwise, it might not go well with you! The foxes can move very, very much faster than we can when we are out of the water. You might end up being their supper if you do not listen to what your parents are saying!" All said that they had listened well.

They went on playing day after day, but finally one of the little ducks became bored. He looked over to the other side and saw that there was the most luscious grass that he had ever seen. I will swim over there, he thought. Why do I have to listen to Papa and Mama? I have never seen sly fox over there! And so he started to swim across the lake.

As he was heading to the other side, his brothers and sisters called out, "Do not swim over there, you must listen to Mama and Papa." He did not listen. When he arrived on the other side there was indeed wonderful, delicate grass! Oh, how good it tasted!

But all of a sudden he heard a "swishshshsh" and his brothers and sisters were suddenly silent. A fox was approaching fast. Now he heard his brothers and sisters call out again, "Run, run, dear little brother!" The little duck had to waddle for his life! Snap! The fox had got hold of his tail feathers, and he felt the bite just as he was back on the water. He could barely escape! What a scare! He had lost many of his nice tail feathers. He looked quite roughed up, but he got away with his life.

Oh, thought the little duck, if I had only listened to Mama and Papa. Just as he thought this, they came swimming as fast as they could. When he was back with them he said, "From now on, I will always listen to Mama and Papa!"

The Search for a Gentle Queen

Once there lived a king in a faraway land in a very beautiful palace. It was a large palace, and he felt very alone in it. So, he decided to get married. He sent out his heralds to call on many royal families to send their lovely maidens to come to his palace. Many came. They were kind and gentle, honest and good. The king was hard pressed to make a decision. How would he know who should become his queen?

One princess came from far away, and she could only visit the palace on one day. But alas, on that very day the king could not be at the palace! When the princess arrived and realized he was not present, she flew into a rage!

She screamed and yelled, she stamped her foot, she kicked the gilded walls, picked up a precious stool and threw it on the floor, swept the dainty dishes off the table so that they shattered on the floor.

Just at that moment the king entered the room. He had returned early from his hunting, and he went to see what all the awful noise was about. When he saw the behavior of the princess, he was aghast! How horrible she sounded, how mean and ugly she looked! She could not possibly become his queen!

So, the princess was sent home in disgrace, and the king chose another princess who was beautiful and kind to be his queen.

*

When creating the stories the evening before their telling, the teacher should have clearly in mind the particular behavior she wants to address in the class as well as the individual or group of children. The teacher then creates specifically out of the immediate connection she has with this child or group of children. The teacher can most certainly also bring into this work a plea to the child's angel to assist and strengthen her efforts. This most assuredly will bring additional healing power. When telling the story in class, the teacher should *not* think of specific children, but offer the story to the whole class. In this way, each child's higher Self can be actively choosing the particular message that the child needs for his healthy development.

The following fourth story of these examples was created to address the behavior of a boy who had decided to become the class clown. He chose to make all kinds of silly faces when story time was about to start in Main Lesson. As teacher, I tried to create a warm, reverential mood for the Main Lesson story each morning. This was unsuccessful because each day the boy turned to the class and made such ugly grimaces that he succeeded in bringing all forty-five children (the size of my class in Germany) to loud laughter. Any attempt to create a mood was frustrated. After speaking with his parents, I decided to create a rather strong story, even a bit stronger than the version below. Then the parents and I waited to see what would happen.

The following day when story time was about to begin, he again turned to the class as he previously had done. I

114

thought with disappointment, "All was in vain." Just at that moment he stopped, turned back, put his hands in his lap, looked at me quietly and waited for the story to begin. (I was so shocked, I almost could not tell the story!) Dear teaching colleagues, you can imagine how I felt. Never again did this boy attempt to make a face. He was able to change from class clown to a totally supportive, eager student. As teacher I could see without a doubt what it means to the child when his higher Self can take hold of a situation. It was a powerful step forward for this child. He did it himself. In this way we work as teachers on a very different level, taking the child's own angel or higher Self into account. The gratitude I felt for being able to experience something like this has continued into the present time.

Being Silly

There was once a little girl and she was always silly. She enjoyed making all kinds of ugly faces. The uglier the better, she thought. She felt that it was especially funny when she made these ugly faces at little children who would get scared and begin to cry.

Her brothers and sisters did not want to be around her anymore because they also got blamed by the other angry moms and dads. So very soon, she had to walk all alone. However, this did not discourage her. She continued to make ugly faces at young children.

Her brothers and sisters were especially embarrassed because on many occasions they overheard other families in their small town say, "Oh, how unfortunate for the poor mother, what a pity that she has such an unkind child." Nobody else thought that the ugly faces were funny. They said, "How terrible the mother must feel."

One day the girl opened her mouth wide to make an ugly face–and then it happened. Her mouth would not close anymore! When she ran to her mother, the mother thought her girl was just making silly, ugly faces again, and she sent her to her room. Big tears rolled down the little girls face. Running back to her mother a second time, she pointed to her open mouth again and again. Soon her mother noticed that the girl was indeed in pain.

They went to the doctor's office. The jaw was very painful. It had to be adjusted by the doctor. After that ordeal the little girl said, "I will never ever make nasty, ugly faces again!" The little girl was totally changed. This made her family very happy.

*

As teachers, we know our students in the classroom. Because of this we can create specific stories that address the particular behavior showing itself. With this approach we are not preaching to the students, which often ruins the mood in the classroom. Rather, the students love these stories because they feel a direct connection to them. Here again work the "imponderables," the underground connection between the soul of the teacher and that of her students.

Writing individual verses

In 1922, in Oxford, Rudolf Steiner presented the lectures contained in *The Spiritual Ground of Education*. Towards the end of the lecture cycle (lecture 8) he spoke about report writing and individual verses:

> The report we make on a child at the end of the school year resembles a little biography, it is like an *aperçu* of the experiences one has had with the child during the year, both in school and out. In this way the child and his parents have a mirror image of what the child is like at this age. Now we also write something else in the report. We combine the past with the future. We know the child and know whether he is deficient in will, in feeling, or in thought; we know whether this emotion or the other predominates in him. And in the light of this knowledge, we make a little verse or saying for every single child in the Waldorf school. This we inscribe in his report. It is meant as a guiding line for the whole of the next year at school. The child learns this verse by heart and bears it in mind. And the verse works upon

the child's will, or upon his emotions… modifying and balancing them.

Thus the report is not merely an intellectual expression of what the child has done, but it is a power in itself and continues to work until the child receives a new report. And one must indeed come to know the individuality of a child very accurately…if one is to give him a report of such a potent nature year by year.[91]

We see here that Steiner originally asks the teachers not only to write a report at the end of each year to give the parents a picture of the experiences with their child during that year, but also to create a verse, a new one every year, that gives a guiding idea, a direction, to the child.

In a conference with teachers on May 25, 1921, Rudolf Steiner speaks directly to them about report writing. He brings up that when writing reports, we need to individualize. All aspects must be discussed and well formulated. It is important to give a true picture of the child, though we must guard against being too blunt or confrontational. He then recommends that the verse be written for each child at the end of the class teacher's report to the parents. "Again for each child there should be a verse below the report that will give a *direction* (emphasis by author) to the individuality of the child, as leitmotif (guiding principle) for the future."

Heinz Mueller, one of the early Waldorf teachers who met and worked with Rudolf Steiner, wrote a creative, helpful, and thorough book called, *Healing Forces in the Word and Its Rhythms.* In it he gives many indications on writing individual verses:

When the Waldorf school was founded in Stuttgart on September 22, 1919, the question came up of how often and in what form reports were to be given…On the report-forms a large space was reserved for what the class teacher had to say about the pupil in question. Rudolf Steiner attached the greatest value to creating as individual a picture of the child as possible. In doing this one was to avoid negative comments. The teacher was to go deeply into the character, the abilities but also the deficiencies and weaknesses of his pupils in as loving a way as he could and to present everything with unfailing goodwill. Only after this should there then follow something of an assessment of what had been accomplished. The picture thus put forward must of course be really faithful and free of distortion. But here also there was to be no suggestion of sitting in judgment or condemnation; rather was there to be shown how an improvement was to be brought about. Whereas with the younger classes this part of the report was to be directed exclusively to the parents, in the middle school one was to address oneself also to the children themselves; without the slightest appeal to ambition, the teacher was to find loving, appreciative words of encouragement even for the dullest of his charges, and in a similar way one could with humor make an impression even on the biggest rascal. Finally the class teacher was to sum up in a verse what he considered should accompany the pupil as inner guidance during the following year.[92]

On May 26, the next day of the conference, Rudolf Steiner indicated succinctly what he expected in the reports. Mueller recalls: "We are agreed that we should write the reports as we did last year. As faithful a picture as possible; at the end once more a verse that can show the individual child the direction in which it should strive."[93]

In English the term "individual verse" is the preferred designation for what often is referred to as the "birthday verse," which to some suggests the verses should be handed out on each child's birthday. This is *not* the case. Rather, what is meant is that the verse would be spoken by the child in class on the day of the week on which he was born–a Monday, Tuesday, and so on.

The teacher introduces individual verses in second grade, not in first grade, to give the teacher time to know her students. New individual verses then should be written every school year.

In the European Waldorf schools the verses are written at the end of the report. In the US, where the reports are sent out after the end of the school year, the verses could be handed out *at the beginning* of the following school year, in September. Every child would receive his or her verse, ideally on the first day of school (or soon after) so that all of the students may speak their verses *on the day of their birth,* every week. Monday morning in the classroom the *Sunday children* begin, followed by the Monday children. *On Friday, the Saturday children follow,* ending the week.

It is always a joy to find out how much the verses mean to the child. Usually the teacher hears about it from a parent. One of the boys in my class at the Sacramento Waldorf school when asked by his mother what he wanted for Christmas said to her, "You know this lady that does calligraphy. I want my verse written in calligraphy very large so I can hang it over my bed." Very heart-warming indeed.

The children teach us how deeply they take in the words that we choose for them when we write these verses. They take them into their feeling and will life. The words activate them. They are deeply meaningful for them. Steiner helps the teachers be aware of the effect their words have:

> Far more than with our thinking the word binds together with our feeling, and far more strongly again with everything that lies in the will. Feeling belongs to a much more unconscious part of the soul than thinking, and willing to a still less conscious part than feeling. For thinking, the words we speak amount to little more than signs. To feeling, they have a far more intimate connection. They join forces with feeling far more closely, and especially closely do they do so with willing.[94]

The students speak their verse once each week of the school year. This is a wonderful way to incorporate repetition. Steiner points out that if teachers wish to reach the feeling and will, they need to remember that "a more unconscious repetition cultivates feeling: fully conscious repetition cultivates the true will impulse."[95]

In the lower grades, and only as long as needed (most likely only during second grade), the teacher speaks the verse together with each child in the beginning of the year. The teacher needs to copy all of the verses in her own book according to the days of the week, so she has them readily before her.

Creating a verse for each child in a large class can be challenging. It is not an absolute that in each case the teacher has to create a new verse, although this is ideal. When I had a class of forty-five children in Germany, as a beginning class teacher I received much-appreciated advice from a seasoned teacher: "Look at the verses other teachers have written, see if one fits well to a particular child, and use it. Feel free to change a couple of lines if need be." In this way I was not under great pressure to have forty-five original verses ready to be included at the end of reports to be handed out on the last day of school. Teachers should always make the greatest effort, but also look for support.

Coming into the upper grades six to eight, I felt the need to pull back as class teacher and to guide more from behind, from the background. I felt it necessary to give the students more space so that more objectivity entered into the relationship, and they could take things on more actively themselves. Therefore, I decided for those upper grades to give a verse to each student that I chose from *time-honored inspirational verse collections*. It is easy to find a verse suitable for each student. By that age the students understand the content and the thought-message. For that reason also, I felt it better not to continue with the personal writing. Teachers need to approach this matter as seems right with their class of children.

Another helpful indication is that the teacher can take the material from the preceding grade (so the children know what you are talking about) as content for the verses in the following school year. This makes things easier, especially if as teacher you were observant enough to write yourself a note when you noticed a child being attracted particularly to one story or another, or in mythology to one god or another, or in history to a historical figure. Steiner pointed out that the verse should give the child *direction*, perhaps to help him *overcome a weakness*. Complementarily, you might want to focus on a *strength* that you see in the child to help him or her to further develop this quality.

When would be a good time for the children to come in front of the class to speak their verse? I found a good time to be after the morning circle, when all children had the chance to move and now could sit still to listen for a while. This worked very well.

Heinz Mueller points out that it is good to do speech exercises with the students before they speak their verses. This makes complete sense. Engage the whole class with speech exercises first. Mueller explains:

> Finally a series of speech exercises is done by the children either singly or together in which the utmost exactitude must be worked for. After this it is time for the report-verses to be said. If one has only a small number of children, one can perhaps let them all say their verses each day. In the very big classes, however, which I myself had, it was a matter of dividing up the children, which led to some interesting groupings. I so arranged it that every child said its verse on the day of the week on which it was born, with the Sunday children leading off on Monday mornings. To begin with, in the earlier weeks of the new school year I myself first said each verse in as good a speech as possible, but later on this was no longer necessary. It was often very astonishing to see how remarkable karmic correspondences showed themselves in the groups arising in this way out of the weekdays of birth.[96]

You can use a particular rhythm in the verse, or move from one rhythm to another. Here the above-mentioned book by Heinz Mueller would be of great help. He gives many examples. He also speaks about the verse in relation to the child's temperament, and how to address it in a healing way.

Steiner gave indications regarding which rhythm would fit optimally to which temperament. His indications given to Heinz Mueller were as follows:

For a sanguine, begin with an anapest; calm it down with an iambic in the following verse.

For a choleric, begin the lines with a spondee; it has power and strength.

For a phlegmatic, the trochee would be good, moving towards the end of the verse or poem to a dactyl.

For the melancholic, the amphibrachus with its beautifully balanced rhythm would be a really excellent choice.

The teacher can limit herself simply to creating verses that address a particular child, if you find using the above rhythms an additional challenge. (If you wish to pursue this further, please go to Heinz Mueller's book).

Below are examples of individual verses from my classes:

Grade 2

Awake be my head
Loving my heart,
Helpful my hand.
Then I will do
All that is right
Truthful and good.
*

Go to, my horse, go to
And if you stumble,
And even tumble
With lame foot
Through marsh and brook,
Never doubt, my horse, go to!

You will reach the castle.
It's waiting for you.
*

To conquer the mighty
Shows goodly strength.
To serve the weak
Shows greater strength
To control oneself
Shows the very best strength.
*

Each day I see
My courage grow
Because I feel
And also know
That what I've done
I have done well.
That's clear for all
To see and tell.
*

With all my strength, as best I can,
I start my work each day again.
That joy may fill my heart and will.
I want to grow up big and strong,
And work and learn my whole life long.
And all I learn I love so much
If what I learn my heart can touch.
*

The flower so bright
The trees so tall,
The grass so fresh,

The blue of the sky,
All things are beautiful I see
And so are things with me.
My hands will work
So clean and neat
And straight to the task
I direct my feet.
*

The light of the sun makes trees grow high
Lets flowers raise their heads with joy,
The light of truth makes strong my heart
That without fear I'll do my part.
*

I'm busy, busy, busy said the bee.
I can't come home for dinner or for tea.
It takes me hours and hours
To visit all the flowers.

I'm glad that I a person be,
Can work in quiet, peacefully
Can clearly hear what others tell.
That's why my work is done so well.
*

From far and high
From star and sky
We bring a light
For us a guide.
Then down we go,
So deep and slow,
We bring the light

And work with might.
*

Michael so brave and true
All my praise I bring to you.
Your strength you lend to all
Who hear your battle call.
To fight for truth and light
Is a deed for a worthy knight.
You can count on me to be there
and to fight in that battle fair!
*

Clear be my mind.
Truth will I find.
Firm will I stand
Wherever I am.
Strong is my hand,
Courageous my heart
In times that are good,
In times that are hard.
*

I dance with the flowers,
I sing with the sun.
The warmth of my heart
I bring everyone.
*

The spirit of the bottle was
Quite powerful you see
And the woodcutter's son
Was small and weak

- Not much of a match, thought he –
Yet unafraid of power and might,
He challenged that spirit quite.
What was the end,
O, don't you know?
His wit was stronger
Than his foe!
*

With helmet of gold
With heart so bold
With mind so clear
Without any fear
Ride forth now, ride
The world is wide.
*

I will watch my word
I will watch my deed
A voice in my heart
To me does speak:
Your word be light!
Your deed be right!
Faintly the voice does speak to me,
Yet I will follow free
I will listen right
And work with might
To do the good.
*

I love to watch the stars at night
To see by day the sun shine bright,

To watch the rain, to smell the air,
To feel the wind play in my hair.

There's so much joy and happiness
A lot to learn, a lot to give.
I love the world , and I'll work hard
For the true and good.
I'll do my part.
*

Quiet on the silvery sea
Swims the graceful swan
Feathers white and light as snow
Peaceful as can be.

His head he holds
So straight and tall
A crown I see with all –
I wonder if within
A hidden prince does dream?

Grade 3

Tender shoots in spring are budding
Trying to unfold their life.
Earth she gives them upright strength.
Sunshine comes and adds his light.
Little plant our love is with you.
Grow now and unfold with pride.
*

Dear Mother Earth, so great and strong

Who tends all things with loving care,
We who come from starry skies
Now thank thee for thy gifts so fair.
Uphold our steps, make strong our deeds,
And bring to life our hidden seeds.
*

A hero bold – so we are told -
Brings goodness to the world.
He fights with giants and with dragons.
I too will be
A fighter free
And watch my actions carefully
That every word will bring accord
That every deed will serve a need
Then I will be that hero free.
*

Offero, wake up and hustle
Where is all your strength and muscle?
Take the staff into your hand
Come, discover bright new land.
Don't listen to the howling storm
Don't fear the water's curling form
Come over, hero, my good friend,
Hear my calling, lend a hand!
*

Christopher helped his brothers.
He carried them on his back
He used his great strength for others
To help, to support, to direct.

The greatest reward was given
To Christopher selfless and good
He found the Lord of the Heavens
And carried Him over the brook.
*

St. Martin rode through ice and snow.
"I hear a voice, good riders, hold."
But no one paid him any heed.
No one perceived the beggar's need.
He stopped his horse and just before
He saw a man, all cold and sore.
He shared his coat to keep him warm,
And on his horse he took him home.
*

Enclosed in my heart is a treasure,
A secret and heavenly light.
It shows me all things in right measure
If deeply I listen inside.
*

A true knight I want to be
All evil before me would flee
A knight so strong and pure
That the world's sorrows I'd cure.

Whom will I choose as guide?
Whose strength brings down the night?
Who fights for truth and light?
St. Michael, the Angel bright.
*

The knights they worked great deeds;
For talk they had no need.
They served the righteous and good.
For justice and truth they stood.
High was their purpose and aim.
I too will fight for such fame.
*

Burning bright my shield and spear
Strong and true my bow.
Against the dragon's fearful might,
To battle forth I go.
With mighty arm and noble heart
Firm steps I fearless take
To conquer him who binds us all
For mankind's sake I rise up tall.

Grade 4

God gave us land in plenty
The strength to plow it, too.
It will depend on many
What work they will to do.
My hands and feet won't rest
I'll always do my best
To change the weeds and wilderness
To corn and fruit to feed the rest.
*

The redwood trees
In heavenly peace

In silence and calm
Have stood all along.
So firm will I stand
As my redwood friends
Unshaken by time
Will I peacefully climb.
*

When God the world created,
He called His angels bright
To work, to form, to shape
In His pure radiant light.

To be His loyal servant,
To work in His pure light,
To follow His commandments,
Like Moses, truly guide.
This be my aim and stride.
*

God shared His greatest splendor
When He created man.
Instilling gifts of grandeur
Since time began.

He gave us speech the fairest
That we can all be heard,
He gave us speech the dearest
To speak out clear, alert.

To show that I am grateful,

I send my voice out far.
If tiny birds can do it,
My voice can reach the stars!
*

Without much work
The rose does bloom.
Gods loving care
Its beauty grooms.

Without much strain
the bird does sing
to God on high
His praise does bring.

But we must rake
and weed and hoe
If in our souls,
a rose should grow.
*

The noble knight
Lives without fear
but well he thinks
and goodness brings.

For silly prattle
has no time,
and idle talk
he thinks a crime.

So tall he stands,
And peace he sends
With patience great
He changes fate.
*

I love the world
and what is in it,
I do enjoy it
Every minute.
But to appreciate
Its wisdom,
To understand
This work sublime,
This be my effort
And design.

Grade 5

Joukahainen went to challenge
Vainamoinen, the wise singer.
Joukahainen was a braggart
With much superficial knowledge.
Oh, what happened, Joukahainen?
Did your challenge not hold up?
"Vainamoinen's primal wisdom
Greater power I know not."
*

The heroes so great
Loved challenging fate.
Adventurous deeds

And marvelous fetes.
Yet wisdom and care
Were also their fare.

Joy in my deeds,
And wisdom to guide them
Then truly I'll meet
Challenge with deed.
*
Trappers showed courage
Through stress and travail
Scouting new land
Blazing a trail.

Many a path
Must still be found.
I welcome a challenge.
On me you can count.
*
Pioneer days long ago
Hard was the work
Long was the day.
Pioneer women,
brave and strong,
tackled all tasks
that came along.
Pioneer women,
Just like you
I love the work

I'm asked to do.
*

Heimdall watched
And Heimdall listened.
Great his patience
Great his calm.
He was first to warn
His brothers when
Ragnarok occurred.
He used his strength
To help the others,
Was quick and
Was alert.
*

Climb the highest mountain
Seek the deepest fountain
With strength and uprightness
With true courage, tireless.
*

Thor with might
His hammer swung
For truth he'd ride
For justice fight.
To Asgard's foes
He travelled so
To rid the lands
Of evil bands.
*

When thunder roars
Here comes great Thor

With mighty strength
Defends the lands.
I, too, will fend
For every friend
That light prevail
And darkness fail.
*

Oh, great Baldur, radiant brother,
You, the light one, you, the gentle
Oh, your death brings endless sorrow
Into Asgard, into Midgard.
We are waiting, oh, bright brother
For thy light to shine before us.
For our future lend us courage
For our earthly deeds give strength.
*

Vainamoinen knew the secrets
He the greatest and the wisest
He who saw all things created
He who knew all related.
Power streams from such a wisdom.
Deep inside this fountain flows
For me, for you, for everyone who knows.
*

Vidar was Odin's silent son
Since primeval time began.
In silence he waited in Asgard's heights
With watchful mind and eager eye.
In silence there ripened
Great wisdom in him.

In silence his future prepared.

But during the time of Ragnarok

His strength in deeds he declared.

Like Vidar I calmly gather my strength

And now step forth with confidence.

*

When the students speak their individual verses one by one in front of the class, the teacher needs to make sure the children speak clearly, slowly, distinctly, and loud enough. The teacher demonstrates first. She helps her students consider melody, rhythm, and intonation. Rhyming in the verses supports their memory. Under no circumstances should the verses be droned on and on, as fast as possible or without a thought.

As Waldorf teachers we know that clear speaking is necessary in order to develop clear thinking. Rudolf Steiner pointed to three steps in early childhood that mark our becoming human: walking, speaking, and thinking. When we move our body, two principles interweave, one form-giving, the other retaining the flow. We witness here the interrelationship of the astral and the etheric body. When we consider speech, not only do two principles interact but the entire human being is involved. The physical body participates with the larynx and vocal chords to make sound audible, the etheric form-giving forces sculpt the consonants, the astral feeling-forces enliven the vowels, and the "I" serves as the overall organizer and overseer of the processes. The "I" induces sense into what we say. The "I" is completely present in our thinking activity, it is the one who thinks.

The art of education

When Waldorf education is called "artistic," it doesn't mean only that the arts are integrated into the lessons. The Waldorf method of educating is itself artistic. *How* the teacher brings the subject matter is the true artistry. Is the teacher's presentation alive and descriptive, characterizing situations so that the child can inwardly picture them, experience them, be present in them? The artistic method differs from any goal-oriented teaching that emphasizes tests and highly values standardized outcomes and measurable results. The artistic method allows for originality and individual results. It focuses on the creative unfolding of each child's possibilities. Steiner speaks of the *art of teaching*. This artistic method draws on the personal creativity of the teacher. It is a path that guarantees the child a free space to become individually active and self-creative in the learning process.

The arts themselves nurture the whole human being and foster creativity and imagination. They bring the soul into movement. For example, through the art of painting, colors seen in nature can begin to speak more distinctly. Through modeling and form-drawing, the element of form becomes more noticeable and stands out more clearly. The art of eurythmy communicates through gestures, and consequently the element of gesture speaks more strongly in nature, also.

The etheric body can be studied through the form element of modeling and sculpting, while the astral body can be studied through color and music. We may say that our soul sings because it is pure music. The true nature of the "I" can be studied through speech. The arts are an expression of our entire being and are therefore also a healing element for us. Healing makes whole.

The arts are an antidote for the massive influence and intrusion of technology into human life. All artistic activity works especially to strengthen the will nature of humans, which is under attack in our information age fed by technology that has become our constant companion, like a "double" of us. We become mere observers of the world, engaging first and foremost our intellect that then directs the will. Steiner points out that this is not the healthy way for the child. It should rather be the will in the child that awakens the intellect. For then the thinking of the child remains flexible, creative, imaginative, and, on the other hand, reality oriented. The arts engage the students with their feeling-willing activity. They heighten awareness of the beauty around them and foster gratitude for the environment. Children come into this world to connect with the living earth. Technology introduced at an early age separates children from this needed connection. This is one of the reasons why the arts are so important in our time. They are the balancing, healing element, for they are a means to reconnect humans of all ages with themselves, their human environment, and the world.

In addition, Steiner speaks of arts that help to individualize the students. He points here to the plastic-pictorial stream: drawing, modeling, form drawing, painting. When a class is chatty and socializes too much, then the teacher might emphasize for a time the arts that individualize. The other artistic stream, the music and speech stream, socializes, brings together, unites. Music is a great uniter, whether in singing or in instrumental music. Speech exercises, verses, and poems spoken in unison also bring the class together. Much can be done with speech activities like alternating individual speakers with groups of students or the entire class. Eurythmy serves both the individualizing and socializing streams, since it has the form element, the color, and the flowing movement element. It is clear that the rhythmic system has to enter into the process so that there is flexibility and breathing in all activities. If the teacher knows about the arts that individualize (form) and the arts that socialize (will) she can bring balancing and healing elements into her lessons.[97]

Which art works on which body?

• Architecture impresses itself on the experience of the physical body.

• Modeling, sculpting, and drawing educate the etheric body.

• Music moves the astral body and speaks to it most strongly, but also color.

• Speech formation reveals the working of the "I".

By engaging the students in form drawing, painting, and eurythmy, we guide the students to connect an inner will activity with outer form. In this way we develop in them a sense for truth, an ability to see the right correspondence between inner and outer.

Eurythmy, a unique element of Waldorf education, is an art that integrates all other arts. In it is movement, speech, music, even form drawing in the choreography, and color in the veils. Eurythmy nurtures and renews life forces, strengthening the etheric.

In the eurythmy lesson the teacher can observe optimally the quality of the child's movement. Are the gestures lazy, silly, tired, or well imitated, expressive, joyfully light? Can the teacher see aggression, anger, destructiveness? Are the gestures well formed? Does the student extend his arms fully or does he lift them minimally and leave hands drooping. The teacher can see whether the child is already well incarnated into his body or not. Is there consciousness, awareness of the movement or not? In the later grades we can see whether the young person can ensoul his movement, or not yet. There are always children who have a difficult time with formed movement, with the focus demanded or with self-control in the tempting open space of the eurythmy room. In the provocations that a eurythmy teacher has to deal with, we can, at times, recognize in the child a cry for help.

Eurythmy is especially healing for today's children. It builds up their etheric forces, which technology and our fast-paced life are wearing down. It would be exceedingly beneficial if eurythmy were in the curriculum at every Waldorf school. The teacher should also realize that eurythmy is not merely a series of movements; its movements open the child's soul to the world. They are listening gestures, bringing the additional benefit that through engaging in it children learn to listen better![98]

If a teacher attends to how language is used in our culture, or even observes herself, she may note how the focus is less and less on the sounds of language and more on the informational content. We focus on the message given. However, when language is used only to convey information, teachers who value speech also as an art form might ask, "How can I gain a living relationship to language itself?" Rudolf Steiner makes us aware that there is an actual being connected with each language, which used to be called the "genius" of the language. These beings work in an immensely creative way. Can we as teachers become aware of these creative beings? Can we raise ourselves to experience the genius of our native language?

Untold wisdom lies in sounds, in words, wisdom deeper than ordinary human understanding. In the Norse legends, the god Odin hung for nine long nights on Yggdrasil, there to undergo an initiation that would give him insight into shaping and forming the human word. During this initiation process he gradually penetrated into the sphere of the cosmic word, there to take hold of the creative wisdom working within it, to bring it down and form it into human language, to form the sacred runes. In this mythology, speech is clearly a gift from the gods. Odin is the genius of language in Norse mythology.

The "I" expresses itself most perfectly in the art of speech. Working with speech is in itself a healing process, because we are using the rhythmic system as we breathe. The "I" itself is the great integrator, integrating our will, feeling, and thinking into the word, into speech. When the teacher's heart-warm connection to the world sounds through her words, the children experience on the one hand the "I"-presence of the teacher and, on the other, they are drawn with interest into the world. Interest is a key element of health because it brings connectedness.

We as teachers need to bring feeling, a soul quality, into speech. We do this when rhythm, meter, melody, and intonation enliven our speaking. When we bring these elements into our language while teaching, our language will live and not be reduced to mere giving of information. The genius of language is the creative force and tremendous wisdom that manifests in language. The teacher should encourage the children to speak with round, full sound, in complete sentences, pronouncing syllables clearly.

The German poet, Friedrich Schiller, as mentioned before, experienced thoughts and words as if inspired by the genius of his language. In his time he could still say, "Thought is my boundless realm and my winged instrument is the word." Steiner picks up on this, pointing to the fact that speech reduced to information may chain human beings to the earthly gravity, instead of lifting him into a 'boundless realm.' Steiner continues: "And whereas through a spiritual world-conception speech could be an ocean into which man's inner being sinks and which could then lift his soul to greater and greater heights, it becomes instead the means of chaining him to the Earth, chaining him to the rigidly limited conditions of earthly existence."[99]

On the other hand, language has structure, grammar. When does the teacher introduce grammar, the working with the structure of the language? At the nine-year change the child becomes ready to find the transition to a more conscious "I"-experience. Now is the right time for teaching grammar and following rules. Grammar gives the child backbone. It has an awakening effect on the student. Therefore, it is good to wait with the formal introduction of grammar until the child is going through the nine-year change, when he is able to separate himself from the language enough to look at its structural elements, beginning with the parts of speech.

Through the extensive language work Waldorf teachers do with their students from first grade on, the "I" can enter in a differentiated manner into the breathing, and from there work to bring health to the metabolic system.

How to cultivate independent judgment?

Up to eleven or twelve years of age, the child still lives strongly in pictures. Then cause-and-effect thinking emerges, which means the astral body is beginning to work, bringing with it the consciousness of the backward stream of time. It is developmentally appropriate to wait with bringing causal connections until the astral body is freeing itself from the connection with the physical body. Consequently, we begin history in fifth grade with biographies, not through cause and effect.

Especially as he goes through the ages of thirteen to twenty-one, the young person wants to form his own judgments of what he meets in life. Forming judgments, discerning, and decision-making are activities of the astral body. Weighing situations is a breathing process, a rhythmic interaction between self and the world, if it is healthy. The more we protect the child from premature judging and criticizing, the better it is for him. If as parent or teacher we push decision-making (which is a form of judging) onto the younger child, what affect does that have? Is it a problem? With the best intentions, parents might encourage a younger child to make his own decisions, convinced this will make him strong and teach him to express himself. Is this not healthy? Here we must be clear: we are actually *weakening* the child, because the astral body, used for judging, discerning, opting, and deciding, is at that younger age still under the influence of the physical body.

This situation is similar to one encountered with the seven-year-old. We can pull on the child's etheric life forces for academic learning at any time, as we know, but there is a price to pay. We siphon off etheric forces too early, when they are still involved in forming and elaborating the organs of the physical body. We draw on the child's regenerative life forces when we encourage academic learning before these forces have completed their bodily task.

We face a similar situation with the astral forces. If we engage the astral forces too early in decision-making, meaning before they have freed themselves from the bodily influences, it can impact the student for the rest of his life. The teacher must understand that before puberty the astral body works *within* the physical body; it has not freed itself. As a consequence, the process of judging, which should be a free and objective process of the soul, becomes bound to the personal influences and whims of the body. Judging with the body's input then becomes habitual. The free, selfless, objective decision-making capacity is not developed, not learned, nor practiced.

A teacher's lack of awareness in this important timing can mean the student develops the habit of judging by personal likes and dislikes, which means he becomes judgmental and prejudiced.

It is essential to wait for the freed astral activity to arise in the soul in which we can bring about a healthy breathing between world and self. This is how a healthy judging process should come about. The astral body is also the carrier of human love and compassion, and these feelings need to be part of every judging activity concerning human social life. When at puberty the young people judge and compare–a process that at first can be very critical–their activity needs to be penetrated by the human love and warmth residing in the astral body. Then gradually compassion for what is human, also for human failing, can develop.

For teachers the main thought to keep in mind concerning the process of decision-making, judging, and discerning is that they should be processes of the soul, inner processes involving the astral body that has freed itself from the automatic physical influence. Rudolf Steiner underscores why this matter is such an important issue for the upper grades:

> On the other hand, if we do not nurture this natural respect for authority, if as teachers we withdraw in order to let the child find out for himself, we force him into making his own judgments prematurely, that is, before what we call his astral body has been born at puberty. We activate this so-called astral-body while it is still engaged in working on the child's physical body. In so doing we impress into his physical constitution what should be imprinted only in the configuration of his soul...Thereby we cause the development of something which will live in the child as harmful factor for the rest of his life. It makes a difference whether he attains the faculty of judgment after due preparation in the fourteenth to fifteen years, when the astral body as the bearer of judgment has been freed, or whether he is trained to judge at an earlier age. In the latter case it is not his astrality, nor his soul faculties which are

drawn upon for making judgments, but his physical body with all its innate properties. Thus the child's temperament, his individual characteristics dependent on the blood, all that calls forth in him sympathies and antipathies, in short all the factors which prevent him from becoming objective, are at the basis of his judging...If we let him judge prematurely, he will use his physical body for this faculty for the rest of his life... Therefore, the best preparation for developing an independent and free human personality is not to cultivate it too early, but to wait for the right moment.[100]

We see how essential it is for teachers to have a clear understanding of the entire process of healthy and not-self-serving decision-making and judging.

Why characterize rather than define?

"Therefore, you ruin the soul of the child if you make him commit to memory ready-made conclusions."[101]

Steiner continues the above statement by emphasizing, "What I am now saying...is of the most fundamental importance for your teaching." Dear friends, what are ready-made conclusions and why do they ruin the child's soul? I think we have examples on end; to give a few: the heart is a pump, the nerve system is a switch board, the nerves are telephone cables, the brain is a computer and so on. These are definitions that can stay with us for the rest of our life. In the teacher education program I asked the beginning students, "What is the heart?" Not surprisingly, most of the students answer "a pump." If such an answer is repeated often enough, we can easily see how we fix the souls of children with such ready-made conclusions. We do not think about them anymore. How many of these do we carry in our soul? We are lucky if, as adults, we notice some of them and are able and willing to do something to loosen them up again!

In lecture nine of *Study of Man* Rudolf Steiner carefully distinguishes between characterization or description and definition. Teachers need to avoid definitions, he says, for they are "the corpses of concepts." They "graft dead concepts right into the bodily nature of the human being when [they] implant dead concepts into him." When the teacher forms a concept and teaches it to the children, "it goes down into the profoundest depths of man's being...The concept makes its way right down into the sleeping soul, and this is that part of the soul that is constantly at work upon the body...the sleeping soul works right into the very forms of the body."[102]

This is enormous! As teachers, as a society, we affect the bodily organs of our children with hard and fixed definitions. Rudolf Steiner associates the "uniformity that has come over humanity" to this fact, that "no true education" was experienced by them.

When we continually give the child definitions, when we say, for example, "A lion is a large tawny-colored cat that lives in prides, found in Africa and northwestern India," then we are "grafting dead concepts into him," says Steiner, and

> you are expecting that at the age of thirty he will retain these concepts in the precise form in which you are now giving them. That is to say: the making of many definitions is death to living teaching. What then must we do? In teaching we must not make definitions but rather must endeavor to make characterizations. We characterize things when we view them from as many standpoints as possible.[103]

When we describe, characterize, and compare and contrast, even we can experience the movement created by living into these words. Below are two animal descriptions that demonstrate very well the difference between definition and characterization. These descriptions were written by two former teacher education students. They bring out the descriptive element beautifully, each story in its own way:

The Lion

Definition: The lion is a warm-blooded mammal. It is a predatory animal, belonging to the family of large wild cats. It lives on the African plains.

Characterization:

When the sun rises early in the morning, and a light breeze bends the tall and dry grasses of the African plains, the young lioness stretches her muscular body and blinks her eyes at the morning sun as she wakes up. She greets the new day with a mighty yawn, and her large, sharp teeth gleam in the sunlight. Then she looks around her and gently nuzzles her young cubs that are snuggled up against her. One by one, they are waking up.

Then the lioness begins the morning task of washing her young ones. But she does not wash them with water, because cats don't like water; rather, she uses her rough, strong tongue, to lick each cub clean. Their soft, tan fur shines as their mother's tongue glides over their little bodies. She removes not only dust and mosquitoes from their fur, but the gentle movements also massage the little ones. When you use a moist washcloth to wash yourself, it feels similar to what those baby cubs experience when they receive their morning bath.

Next it is time for breakfast, and today the lioness is going to teach her cubs how to hunt for their food. Up until today, she has always left her cubs, hidden in the safety of a large bush while she went out in search of food, but today, for the first time, the little ones may accompany her. You can imagine how the excitement grows among the cubs. They begin to tumble about, and jump on each other in sheer anticipation. But the lioness lets them know that today they must watch her carefully. If they are too noisy, they will chase the prey away! The cubs promise to be on their best behavior, because they want to be allowed to participate in the hunt.

The lioness begins to stake out the area, and she decides to hunt at the stream, where most of the animals will gather to drink. There she will find the best prey, and have the easiest hunt. They set off on the journey. The little cubs can barely control themselves and every once in a while one will try to do something to tug on his brothers and sisters, but as they near the stream, the lioness gives a swish of her mighty tail to scold the cubs and remind them to behave like proper and kingly lions today.

The closer they get to the stream, the more the air of the savannah begins to change. The breeze feels cooler now and the dry, brown grasses which they have been treading through give way to green shrubs and trees. The lioness uses her keen nose to scout out the scents of the different animals which are gathered at the stream. The cubs learn from watching their mother, but they can't quite distinguish between the different animal's scents yet. They can just smell that many animals are there. The lioness can tell that there are zebras, water buffalos, birds, and antelope. As they approach closer, they move ever so quietly and slowly, taking large, but careful steps, as to not give their presence away. The grasses hardly move as their lithe bodies glide between them.

Then the lioness stops in her path, and the little ones follow her. She now watches intently to spy which of the animals would be easiest to hunt. The antelope are too quick for the cubs to catch; the water buffalo are too large. For today she decides on the zebras. After watching carefully, she notices an older zebra, that seems to be moving slower than the other ones and it becomes her target. The lions haven't eaten in a while and their stomachs are growling in anticipation of food. The old zebra moves closer to the location of their hiding spot. Quickly the lioness charges out from the brushes, with five little excited lions in tow. They try to encircle the zebra from all sides, but the zebra gallops in zigzags about to escape. The lioness could easily run down her prey, but today she wants the cubs to learn how to hunt, so she steps back to let them try. They are still unorganized and too playful to know how to hunt precisely yet.

It is the zebra's lucky day as it escapes by jumping through the encircling cubs. Quickly it gallops off to rejoin its herd, while the young cubs return to their mother with disappointed faces. This was their first attempt and the young lions have learned that they still have much to learn about hunting. They will try again and again for weeks to come, until they become skillful enough to fend for themselves.

Although this description would be on the young side for a fourth grade animal block, all of the elements Steiner recommends are contained in it, including his recommendation that there should always sound through the presentation the relationship to the human being himself.

The Cow

Definition: The mature female of any bovine animal, especially of the domesticated species. The cow is a ruminant. It has four stomachs which work on the digestion of its food, and its intestines are 22 times as long as the animal's body. The human being takes in about $1/40^{th}$ of his own weight in nourishment daily but the cow needs $1/8^{th}$.

Characterization:

It was a warm summer evening and the night breezes were just beginning to blow across the land, cooling it from the day's heat. The sun, not quite set, illuminated the sky with brilliant colors. On the farm the animals were settling down for the night and milking time was just beginning. The cows' heads hung low and bobbed up and down as they followed the narrow path which led from the pasture to the barn.

Each animal moved forward at a slow unhurried pace. For the cow, she cannot be hurried and to see her running is to see something quite out of place. She is slow and not built for speed. She has a great large head and massive body with very thin legs. She is dreamy and she loves to eat.

The path the cows move along ends at the barn where the bright electric lights burn. The cows enter one by one and each cow goes to the same stall each night. There they find waiting for them the sweet hay and grain mix of oats, barley and corn that they love so much. Immediately the cows begin to swallow their food, for a cow does not chew the food and then swallow it like humans, but she swallows it and brings it up again to chew. This is known as chewing the cud, and animals that eat like this are called ruminants. This way of eating has really something to do with the four stomachs a cow has. We can see how the cow has adapted to chewing by her long jaw and if we looked inside of her mouth we could see her huge back teeth.

So when we see her lying so peacefully in the fields, we know she is really working hard digesting the meadow grasses she has eaten. One could look at a cow as a walking stomach. One result of this digesting is milk. Now the cows, having begun their evening meal await the farmer.

Quietly he comes down the aisles with the milkers. The milkers each have four suction cups attached by hoses to a big stainless steel container. Gently the farmer attaches the suction cups to each of the four teats of the cow. The suction in the hoses draw the milk out into the container, and the barn is full of the rhythmical sound of the milkers going swoosh swoosh, – swoosh swoosh. Now a cow is quite relieved to be milked, for throughout the day her udder has grown very large and full. Oftentimes, if a farmer is late for his milking, the cows will all wait at the barn door mooing loudly to be let in. This mooing is a thick, heavy earthy sound. There are some milk cows that will milk out as much as three to four gallons of milk in one milking. Imagine that! That is a lot of milk to be carrying around. It is no wonder she moves so slowly. The cow will not only give this much milk in the evening but she will also give this much milk in the morning as well!

What does the farmer do with all that milk? He and his family drink some of the milk, of course. The farmer makes butter from the cream that rises to the top of the milk bottle; he also makes cheese. The rest he can sell so others have milk too. When it is sold it is made into cheese, butter and yogurt as well, and then we find it in the stores where we can buy it.

After all the cows have been milked and they have eaten all their food, they are let out of the barn. The farmer comes down the aisles with shovel and wheelbarrow to scoop up the cow's droppings. He takes this rich manure and puts it back out on his fields, where it enriches the soil so well.

The cows having been let out of the barn into the cool summer night, find the stars shining brightly above them. Together they gather close, some standing, some lying down, and they begin their night's rest, peacefully and tranquilly.

These two completely different approaches are both strongly descriptive. The reader can picture every situation from beginning to end. Pictorial description is one of the artistic elements in teaching. With it children become engaged and are drawn into the subject, and they are practicing their inner picturing ability. The approach sets the stage for imaginative and creative thinking, a lifelong need, and it is also essential for such skill development as reading comprehension and problem-solving of all kinds.

We experience easily how alive such characterizations and descriptions are, and how easy to remember. As teachers we also immediately understand how much more work such preparation entails, not just in the creating but also in the free delivery, completely without notes. What Waldorf education requires can be challenging for the teacher but is ten times more rewarding for both children and teachers.

Part III: The path of the Waldorf teacher

The teacher's inner life

It can become amply clear to awake individuals in our present time that as a global human society, we can continue to evolve in a healthy manner only if we learn to live together in a mutually appreciative and supportive way. As human beings, we are not born as examples of perfection; instead, every human being is a work in progress. This means, however, that humans when incarnating on this earth do not only have to work in the outer world to make a living but also need to work on themselves to bring about the necessary healthy personal and social life. From the time we are born until we die, we human beings acquire skills that we need in our relationship with the outer world. We also need skills in our relationship with each other, and in the relationship to ourselves.

This calls first of all for inner courage to look at our own strengths and weaknesses with honesty. We need to approach our weaknesses with just as much enthusiasm as we do with some outer task, like fixing a car or a bike, preparing a meal or baking.

What would looking at ourselves with total honesty entail? A willingness to take up a practice to acquire self-knowledge on one hand, and on the other to embark on a path of self-development. How do I work on the weaknesses that I see in myself? Often we have the chance to learn from the people around us through their reactions to what we do or say. We need to pay attention to what comes toward us.

Teachers need to become conscious of their effect on their human environment. Especially as teachers, we need to become aware of our strengths and weaknesses, because they affect the children we teach. This is another unique aspect of Waldorf education that from the beginning of the festive opening of the first Waldorf school in 1919, Rudolf Steiner considered contemplative, meditative practice to be part of the Waldorf teachers' daily work.

As Waldorf teachers we have the great opportunity to work together in a school environment without a principal. Steiner wanted the teachers to develop a new way of working, in which each teacher would be fully engaged and feel, "This is my school, and the full responsibility for the quality of the work rests with *all* teachers. I am co-responsible for the well-being of the school, the parents, and, above all, the children." Working in this co-responsible way, each teacher will go the extra mile. It must be realized that this way of working on an even par with one another acknowledges that there is a higher Self within each individual, immensely capable, immensely committed.

As teachers, we should discover this higher Self in us, for this is the selfless self, capable of working for the common good, while our self-seeking, self-interested self is what needs to be transformed! This self-transformation is necessary for working harmoniously with colleagues, on the one hand, and having the best possible impact on the whole child, on the other. The work we do on ourselves will show itself clearly in the teachers' meetings, in our constant good will, our patience, our willingness to listen with warm attention and carefully consider and weigh the suggestions proposed by our colleagues.

Meditation or contemplation and practice are activities that are not always easy to sustain, because they call for will and commitment. A common pattern is that an individual begins with good intentions and after a few weeks he or she starts to find excuses for why it is not possible to meditate on that particular day. Then the practice lessens until the effort comes to an end. After some months or years the person might become inspired and try again.

A teacher hopefully can come to the place where inner practice is as important to her as outer exercise. In other words, the practice we take on as teacher or parent must become a habit. What does it mean to become a habit? All habits connect with our etheric time-body. And just as we become hungry at twelve o'clock when we are used to eating at that time, so do we feel the need to practice, and this also needs to be done every day at the same time. Establishing a rhythm is helpful.

When practice has become a habit, we need it, we wish it, and we cannot be without it.

The little exercise with big impact

One little exercise that is great for every adult can really help us to get into a rhythm. Taking up the recommendation by Rudolf Steiner to concentrate on the time before going to sleep and on the time when waking up, we focus on gratitude and trust. In the evening before going to sleep, we fill our soul with gratitude for our families, friends, career, health, and all the gifts we can think of, including that we are alive on this beautiful earth! This exercise should make us aware how others have helped us grow and mature and how they have changed us. It awakens in us true appreciation for the other human beings that have come into our lives. We gain the insight that none of us can develop without others. From the practice of this exercise, gratitude gradually becomes the way we approach all things in life.

In the morning on waking, the soul should be filled with trust. Trust that all that comes to us on that day is meant for us, all the good things, all the challenging things. Those actively working with this exercise begin to understand that life has purpose, that what meets us has meaning for us. They lose the need to blame others for difficulties experienced. Rather, they begin to ask questions: What am I to learn from this? The individual becomes more conscious of her path through life, of her destiny. Fear can be overcome because we discover that there is guidance. Life is not happenstance. We each become more aware of our own self–get to know ourselves more. So many discoveries can be made with such a "simple" exercise. It will change lives because it transforms our attitudes towards other human beings.

This exercise, which does not have to take long, is a great way to come to regular practice. As teachers, we affect children, parents and colleagues with our inner attitudes. We may become aware of unresolved issues in ourselves. Our "stuff" whatever it may be hinders our effective and harmonious working with colleagues.

The pedagogical law

Rudolf Steiner made the teachers aware in numerous ways of the effect they have on their students. He spoke of the teacher's temperament, and about the effects of a teacher's soul life on students. He also spoke of the "pedagogical law," as he called it, being a guide for teachers to understand how they affect their students. He presented this pedagogical law to doctors and therapeutic teachers in 1924, in the *Curative Education* course.[104] This law is a gem, unique to Waldorf education. It makes abundantly clear why meditative practice is a necessity for every teacher: The teacher's effect on a child must be a healthy one.

I have picked two excerpts by Steiner from many. The first one reminds us of the teacher's impact on the child, and the second one addresses the pedagogical law specifically:

> Children are aware, whenever we do something in their environment, of the thoughts behind a hand gesture or facial expression. Children intuit them: they do not, obviously, interpret facial features, since what operates instead is a much more powerful inner connection between child and adult than will exist later between adults. Consequently, we must never allow ourselves to feel or think anything around children that should not be allowed to ripple on within the child. The rule of thumb for all relationships in early education must be this: Whether in perception, feeling, or thought, whatever we do around children must be done in such a way that it may be allowed to continue vibrating in their souls.[105]

Specifically about the pedagogical law, Rudolf Steiner says:

> Here we encounter a law, of the working of which we have abundant evidence throughout all education. It is as follows. Any one member of the being of man is influenced by the next higher member… and only under such influence can that member develop satisfactorily. Thus, whatever is to be effective for the development of the physical body must be living in the etheric

body–in *an* etheric body. Whatever is to be effective for the development of an etheric body must be living in an astral body. Whatever is to be effective for the development of an astral body must be living in an ego; and an ego can be influenced only by what is living in a spirit-self…If you find that the etheric body of a child is in some way weakened or deficient, you must form, you must modify, your own astral body in such a way that it can work upon the etheric body of the child, correcting and amending it.[106]

The pedagogical law shows that each one of the teacher's members has an influence on the next lower member of the child:

Teacher	Child
The teacher's etheric body _____	on the child's physical body
The teacher's astral body _____	on the child's etheric body
The teacher's "I" _____	on the child's astral body
The teacher's Spirit Self _____	on the child's ego

The spirit Self of every human being will only come to full development in the future. Since this is the case, the child's "I" can only be approached indirectly, by addressing his angel. Therefore, the child's "I" remains free from direct influence.

The "I" of every human being must be respected as the realm of freedom. In this sphere, humans are open for new impressions and experiences, for new learning, in each incarnation. In this sphere destiny speaks. The other subtle members are influenced, as seen above, by the next higher member.

The question for the Waldorf teacher then becomes, "How can I work on my own subtle bodies so that they may have a healing and strengthening effect on the child?" Here we come back to the challenge of self-knowledge and self-development.

The teacher's etheric body works on the child's physical body. What can she do to strengthen her etheric body? This strengthening can occur through enough sleep, good daily rhythm, and a healthy lifestyle that includes nature walks and natural foods. In addition, the teacher can strengthen her own etheric body with moods of joy, positivity, confidence, inner calm, and centeredness. This will impart to the child a feeling of trust and security. Artistic activities, especially modeling, form drawing and eurythmy, strengthen the etheric body. Regular meditative practice empowers a teacher's whole being, because how human beings think and what they think directly influences their physical health.

The teacher's astral body is strengthened by interest in and love for the world, in the subjects and in all activities executed in the classroom, and for being a teacher. The practice of the six essential exercises [see next section] brings equanimity and balance into the emotional life. The teacher's astral body can impact her students strongly. Strong emotions can throw boulders even onto the teacher's own path, and can then weaken the etheric life forces of her students. We teachers need to learn to control anger, envy, impatience, gossiping, the list goes on and on. The undeveloped astral body is a great egoist.

Our "I" has a healing influence if we have progressed at least somewhat beyond the pervasive egoism (selfishness) so rampant in our time. Our higher "I" is the one that can heal, that can show compassion, that can appreciate, that can give form to our own life, our relationships, and our classwork. Form and organization have such a clean, clear effect! Our "I" is our presence, our attention; it is our selfless supporter.

Understanding the pedagogical law gives Waldorf teachers insight to benefit the life and health of their students. The pedagogical law works in us personally also; our higher member affects the one below. If we just let ourselves go, then the unhealthy effect of the upper member will harm the member below.

As teachers we can also deduce from working with the pedagogical law that in our present time it is, strictly speaking, not acceptable anymore to work together with others without being on a path of self-development. We need to gain at least some self-knowledge and wake up to the effect we have on the people and situations around us. Otherwise, we let those in our environment suffer the brunt of our uncontrolled emotions.

The essential exercises

We work on our subtle members optimally when we start with Steiner's six essential exercises. They are designed to harmonize and strengthen our soul forces, our thinking, feeling and willing. If we choose not to engage in any work on ourselves, it may pose a difficulty for faculty meetings. Then, the danger lurks at times that a teacher unloads her uncontrolled emotionality to the detriment of the meeting. It is an imposition on the other faculty members if I do not work on controlling my thoughts, feelings and actions. In addition to strengthening control over our own soul forces, these exercises also support our social interactions, in that we are asked to practice open-mindedness and positivity. Faculty meetings are a perfect place to practice these!

Six essential exercises:

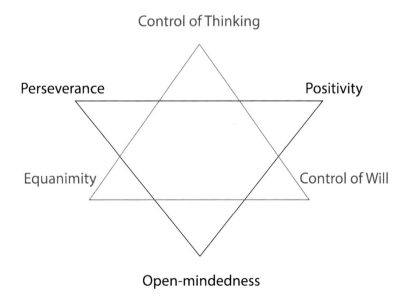

The three red exercises (above) focus on the healthy strengthening of our own thinking, feeling, and willing. The black triangle exercises focus on our social environment. Are we open-minded enough to listen to the other person's thoughts, taking in fully what is being said, without an inner personal reaction, positive or negative?

Are we positively inclined to those working with us? Are we supportive of them? Are we willing to focus on their numerous positive aspects even though we can see in them, as in us, that there are weaknesses? Positivity does not mean everything is positive, but that we emphasize the positive, focus on *it*, rather than focus on the negative: that we see the glass half full, rather than half empty. Here we are working in the realm of feeling.

Perseverance is reliability. When we offer to take on a job for the faculty, will we carry through? Can we persevere? Can we promise to ourselves to work on this or that, and can we then persevere or do we soon give up? Here we are dealing with our will. A big question for us is this: Can we persevere with these six exercises?

These essential exercises are powerful and fairly quickly show some transformative results if done with inner seriousness.

Begin with the exercise to strengthen the force of your thinking. Set yourself the task that *you* decide what you will think for the time-span of a few minutes. Take an insignificant object that does not attract your attention naturally, so that you can learn to give attention. Take a pencil, a key, a blackboard, any simple object. You need an object that you can describe. Look at the object's form, color, material, construction, function. For example, begin by looking at a whole pencil carefully. How long is it, how thick, how smooth? Is something written on it? Does the writing come in different font sizes? After you have looked at the pencil carefully, close your eyes and begin to describe verbally (that is a help at first): the pencil is yellow, made out of inexpensive wood, about seven or eight inches long. It is thin, six sided, and looks new. Its graphite, showing at the tip of the pencil is unused. The wood around the tip is cone shape; it is clean. There is writing on the pencil and a number. At the back is a silver clamp with an eraser. You can certainly go into what the pencil is used for (Do not get lost, though. Stay with the pencil!) or how it is made and so on. See if you can think your thoughts without interruption, without getting distracted. Can you manage three minutes?

The second is a will exercise. It strengthens your will, your determination, and your discernment. Since you are now engaging in a will exercise, it is about executing an insignificant deed: Pull your ear, your nose, turn your ring. Do something that can easily be performed wherever you may be. Set yourself the task of turning the ring on your finger first thing when you wake up in the morning. Tell yourself in the evening that you wish to do so. That helps. Of course, you may forget again and again, but there comes a time when you do this first thing every morning. When you have established it then do this exercise at a time that you have decided upon. See if you can remember to do your exercise then. This is a really effective exercise.

The equanimity exercise is practiced when the occasion lends itself. Work on staying calm and keeping your head clear; emotions should not take over. If they do, you cannot think straight. This challenging exercise brings the astral body under a healthy control.

The remaining three exercises are practiced to create a healthier and more harmonious social life. You can practice them only when you are with others, where you can always check your own reactions.

After practicing the thinking exercise for a few weeks (at least four), add the will exercise. In this way you can proceed, adding the other exercises to your practice. Practicing is more important for the teacher than jumping immediately into meditation, because these exercises effect the change that can make a successful meditative practice possible. Working with these exercises, you begin to feel that you are becoming master of your own house. You can work with these six essential exercises for years. Rudolf Steiner recommends to work with them every day later on as a lead in to your meditative work, which is to follow. Good luck with these great exercises!

By working on yourself as teacher, you begin removing debris that hinders access to your own higher self, the spiritual world, and spiritual beings. Waldorf teachers can then look at Steiner's suggestion to connect with the children's angel beings, who are their eternal guides. Steiner's recommendation from the beginning of the first Waldorf School in Stuttgart was for teachers to work together with the beings of the third hierarchy, the angels, archangels, and archai. When the teacher strives to work to include spiritual beings, he is working for a healthy social future.

A healthy future

Rudolf Steiner focuses on building a healthy earth environment and healthy human culture. We meet his work in biodynamic agriculture, medicine, education, therapeutic education, art and art therapy, and much more. For humanity he envisions a future in which human interactions occur in a socially and spiritually sensitive way. In this shaping of the future, education plays a major role. One task of a healing education is to keep humanity conscious of the fact that human beings have a soul and a spirit, and that human beings have both sensible and super-sensible capacities and bodies.

Rudolf Steiner pointed to three new human abilities to be developed in the present time and into the future through conscious, individual effort. In the future humanity will need the following:

• An *economic environment* in which brotherhood, human love, and compassion in all financial matters will be the guiding principles.

• A *rights sphere* in which "justice for all" will become a reality. How? In the future a true encounter will reveal to us the other's individual divinity. Religion (*re-ligare* means *re-connecting*) will then be a direct experience occurring in the meeting of the other. The spiritual core of the other will be a direct perception. This will make human encounters a true communion.

• *A sphere of spiritual life* in which freedom and personal responsibility will be the foundation of a healthy social life. Human beings will realize their position as a bridge between the temporal and the eternal, between the sensible and the supersensible. Freedom goes together with responsibility, because freedom cannot succeed unless I am aware and care how my actions affect others.

Festive event

Before the opening of the first Waldorf school in Stuttgart, Germany, in August 1919, Rudolf Steiner celebrated a festive event with the original teachers. He spoke of this opening as "a true cultural deed" and as the "renewal of modern spiritual life."[107]

He indicated further that opening the Waldorf school and working in it as a teacher would pose a different and greater task. It would be a moral-spiritual task, and the very first thing the teachers would need to reflect upon would be "how to create a connection from the very beginning between their activity and the spiritual worlds." He encouraged the teachers to see the opening, "as a festive act within the cosmic order," that they should realize that they need to "see each other as human beings brought together by karma."

Steiner also made clear who the being is that stands behind this education. It is Michael, who is the ruling Spirit of our Time, the one who sends his inspirations to humanity to re-spiritualize human life.[108] This is currently a necessity in order to save humanity from another "fall," this time into the subterranean realm of electricity and magnetism.

When we contemplate the beginning of Waldorf education, we understand in our heart of hearts what Steiner meant by "festive act within the cosmic order," for the opening was an event in which the presence of spiritual beings was certainly sensed by all those who participated.

At one point in the festive event, Steiner asked those present to put down their pens, listen, and only take in what he continued to bring to them in this spirit. Those gathered later spoke of their experience as being lifted into the presence of those higher beings.

If these powerful perspectives connected with the festive beginning live in us, then the danger will be avoided that Waldorf education becomes merely a method. We have to realize that Steiner connected this education with the working of the third hierarchy! As he said:

> We can accomplish our work only if we do not merely see it as a matter of intellect and feeling, but, in the highest sense, as a moral-spiritual task. Therefore, you will understand why, as we begin this work today, we first reflect on the connection we wish to create from the very beginning between our activity and the spiritual worlds. Thus we wish to begin our preparation by first reflecting upon how we connect with the spiritual powers *in whose service and in whose name each one of us must work*." [emphasis added]. Steiner then makes the teachers aware that they should understand the introductory words "as a kind of prayer to those powers who stand behind the teachers with Imagination, Inspiration and Intuition."[109]

He continued by saying that the teachers should not view the founding of this school as an "ordinary everyday occurrence, but instead regard it as a ceremony held within the Cosmic Order." He then thanked the "good spirit" who inspired Emil Molt who made the school physically possible. This "good spirit" is Michael.

Rudolf Steiner then guided the teachers through the stunningly beautiful, deeply moving meditation known as the *Teachers' Imagination*. With this imagination Rudolf Steiner was laying the foundation stone for the Waldorf school movement into the hearts of the teachers. It is a response to the question: How do we connect with the third hierarchy? Steiner built that bridge for all Waldorf teachers present and future, right then and there, making them aware that the beings of the third hierarchy wish to work with us and that behind each one of the teachers his angel is standing.

When you live with heart and soul in the *Teachers' Imagination*, you experience that this spiritual foundation stone of Waldorf education was laid into the hearts of the teachers in the presence of Michael, uniting them and all following Waldorf teachers in a common bond with each other and with the beings of the third hierarchy. When we actively and consciously seek this connection, strong healing forces, a spiritual life stream, can flow into our educational work.

Years after the event the teachers Herbert Hahn (in 1967) and Caroline von Heydebrand (in 1938) left written descriptions of this imagination. The angel, whose concern and task is the individual human being, accompanies him through all lifetimes.

The Teachers' Imagination

Behind each teacher her angel is standing, laying both of his hands upon her head. With this gesture he allows strength to flow through the whole being of the earthly human individual entrusted to him, filling her with confidence and commitment. This strength is creative power that awakens the imaginations needed in the classroom.

We can experience the archangels in a circular sweep above the heads of the group of teachers weaving together the offering of each teacher, brought to life through the meeting with her angel, with the offering of the others in a great, uniting gesture. They form and shape what they thus weave together into a sculpted vessel. A chalice is formed above the heads of the teachers. It is composed of a special substance: it is formed out of courage. The archangels allow creative forces of inspiration to stream to the teachers for their work.

Out of their sphere of light an archai appears, lingers for a moment, and having perceived the chalice brings his gifts of light-filled wisdom and allows a drop of this substance to fall into this chalice. This drop of light is given by the "Good Spirit of our Time," by Michael, who stands behind the founder and the founding of this school. We can experience this gift of light in the intuitions awakened by this archai to enhance the teacher's educational insight.

In this way the teachers may work with the beings of the third hierarchy, receiving strength, courage, and light for their work with the children. The third hierarchy will manifest in the awakened imaginations, inspirations, and intuitions.[110]

We can experience the gifts we receive from working together with the beings of the third hierarchy as the healing medicine for the Waldorf movement. We must realize, however, that it is in our hands, individually and together, to what degree these forces may continue to stream into the educational work.

In that the connection with the third hierarchy was established by Rudolf Steiner at the first school's opening, we may feel free to ask these beings for their help as we find our way in guiding our students. A good time to address these beings was also suggested by Rudolf Steiner:

in the evening before individual meditations

and in the morning after meditations.

We see how this would start the day and end the day with a consciousness of working together with these beings.

The child's angel

The teacher can also turn to the angel of a child, especially when she is trying to find answers for how to meet children who have particular and special needs and challenges; when the teacher is wondering: How should I approach this particular child? Where exactly lie the challenges, in the physical, etheric or astral body? In my years as class teacher, I struggled at times to see where the challenges originated that I noticed in a child. I often turned for help to the child's angel, asking him *to bring to my attention* where I should look and what I could do to assist the child. These were questions that I put to the angel of the child, and in addition to my own angel (just to make sure that one of them would answer!).

The angel of the child is, of course, very interested in helping since he accompanies this particular individual throughout all of his or her incarnations. Angels have the task to accompany one human being continuously through all lifetimes. We can imagine then that the angel wants this human child to have all the chances and opportunities karmically possible in order to be optimally prepared for adulthood, when change is far more difficult. The angel knows this growing human being intimately and can therefore be of ultimate help to the teacher. We must listen for the answer as approaching us not from the outside as they do here in the earthly world; *the answer approaches us from the inside*, as if suddenly the light went on. We gain a sudden insight. I have found the following prayer a great help in approaching angel beings:

Prayer to the Angel or Genius

"You, my heavenly friend, my angel, who has led me to the earth and who will lead me through the gate of death into the spirit-home of the human soul, you who knows the path since millennia, do not cease to enlighten me, to strengthen me, to advise me, so that I will emerge from the weaving fire of destiny as a stronger destiny vessel and will learn to fill myself ever more with the meaning of the divine world goals."

Rudolf Steiner said of this prayer:

> The prayer is a direct invocation of the human soul to his angel. Every human being has his angel, his individual guiding being who constantly accompanies the individual and who gives this earthly human being out of the immediate perception of the total web of destiny the right impulses and indications–if this soul wishes to take them up. The angel knows this human soul intimately, its strivings, its tasks, needs, and fears. He grasps this soul with its entire being in the same way that he grasps the spiritual world with its laws

167

and possibilities, and he helps and guides the human soul on its assigned paths.

Meditation and the teacher

All of these practices mentioned are part of the meditative work of the teacher. Steiner gave many different meditations. He also often gave guidance as to how to approach meditation in a fully conscious way according to our present day consciousness. For now it is and should be the meditant himself who is in charge of his meditational work. This is what makes this work *the only really free deed we can accomplish.*

Rudolf Steiner's insights into meditation in *The Mystery of the Trinity* help us understand what meditative practice is or can be in our present time:

> We should not think mystically about meditation, but then neither should we think of it lightly. It must be completely clear what meditation is in the modern sense. It also requires patience and inner energy of soul. Above all there is something else that belongs to meditation, something that no one can ever give to another human being: the ability to promise oneself something and then keep that promise. When we begin to meditate we begin to perform the only really fully free act in human life…Meditation is an essentially free act. If we are able to remain true to ourselves despite this freedom, if we promise ourselves, not another but ourselves, that we will remain faithful to this meditation, then that is, of itself, an enormous power in the soul.[111]

Anyone wishing to meditate can do so by placing a sentence or an image before his or her mind's eye and putting full focus on it. This is also how teachers can approach some of the challenging thoughts when working with the *Study of Man*. Rudolf Steiner continues to give us insight into this way of working by offering this entry into meditation:

> I would like to draw your attention to meditation in its simplest form. I can only deal with the basic principles today…An idea or image, or a combination

thereof, is moved into the center of our conscious-ness…Everything depends on us gathering together our whole life of soul in order to concentrate all our powers of thinking and feeling upon the content of the meditation. Just as the muscles of the arm become strong as we work with them, so too soul forces are strengthened by focusing them on a meditative content again and again.[112]

Those who work consistently with the *Study of Man* lectures understand them to be material for meditation. These lectures are written not only to be grasped by the intellect. We can work with challenging concepts given by Steiner in these lectures in a meditative way.

We can take the approach mentioned, meditating on select sentences. For example, we read a sentence such as, "The task of the teacher seen in a soul-spiritual way is to integrate harmoniously the soul-spirit of the child with the living body." Then we ask ourselves: What does that mean? How can I understand it? What is expected of me as teacher? How can I go about harmonizing these two very different entities? When we contemplate what we read, we discover numerous levels of meaning.

Words for the teachers

At end of the fourteen lectures of *Study of Man*, Steiner guides our consciousness again toward the essential qualities needed by the teacher by concluding with this motto:

Imbue yourself with the power of imagination.

Have courage for the truth.

Sharpen your feeling for responsibility of soul.

He points out that the teacher needs imagination, courage for the truth, and a feeling of responsibility.

Imbue yourself with Imagination: Transform your thinking, be process oriented, not outcome and product oriented. Rather, learn to characterize, describe, and bring pictures. Have ideas, be creative!

Have courage for the truth: Seek the truth, do not remain caught up in personal sympathies and antipathies, not in personally preferred opinions. In other words, work on your feeling and emotional life, work to liberate it from your physical body, from egoism and from the inclination to wish to fit in and take the easiest way possible.

Sharpen your feeling for responsibility of soul: Not my will but Thy will be done. The selfless, concerned, loving care for children, and for the other companions along this path of life. What is my responsibility? What are the needs in this situation? How can I contribute in a healthy way?

These reflections can be put in this way:

Dear Teacher,

Be an artist in your whole being and in all that you do.

Be a seeker for the truth, penetrate life, and penetrate the material you teach.

Be aware of the karmic relationship between you and the children, between you and your colleagues, in some respects even between you and the parents.

Be an artistic, imaginative individual who seeks the truth, takes responsible action, and faces the world courageously.

At the same time that Steiner gave the lectures in *Study of Man* in the morning, he followed them with the lectures on *Practical Advice to Teachers*. In these lectures Steiner presents us with four principles saying, *"I would like you to keep steadfastly to the following four principles,"* [emphasis added].

1. The teacher must be a person of initiative in everything that he does great and small.

We can hear in these words: Be a teacher of initiative, be inwardly active, be wakefully present in all that you do. This is a call we need to hear in our present time. Be not just onlookers who stand passively aside but be individuals who wish to participate. Individuals who hear the call in Rudolf Steiner's verse: "Victorious Spirit, flame through the impotence of irresolute souls!" (*Anweisungen*, German Edition, GA 42, 81). Be an individual who hears and feels the new Michaelic wind that has begun to blow. Here we are addressed on the level of our "I".

2. *The teacher should be a person who is interested in the Being of the whole world and of humanity.*

Reflecting on these words we may think: Interest leads to love. Interest leads to cherishing the other person. It opens the world for us. The natural kingdoms speak to us in their own language when we begin to show interest in them. Our interest in the child is a solid foundation for her; it gives her courage to open up, it gives her life-long security and trust in herself. Here we meet the activities necessary for a healthy astral body.

3. *The teacher must be a person who never makes a compromise in his heart and mind with what is untrue.* Truth strengthens our etheric body. Without truth in our heart and mind, we cannot approach the spiritual world, for there only truth counts. There we cannot hide behind an outer façade. It is gone. And therefore we may hear sounding forth in our heart: Be authentic, be true to yourself. Dare to be a self-responsible individual. Dare to stand for what is true. Then you can enliven the etheric body.

4. *The teacher must never get stale or grow sour.*

In the *Education of the Child* Steiner states: "Joy hatches healthy organs." There we have a clear indication of the effect of joy on our students. Keep both joy and inner enthusiasm alive. Keep an inner freshness, look forward to your students every day. Bring gratitude to your consciousness, gratitude for the amazing opportunity to work with an education like Waldorf education. Here we work in the physical realm.

Steiner has given numerous other exercises and meditations for teachers that I am not mentioning here. You can find several of them in his various lectures for teachers. The actual teachers' meditations are usually handed to teachers when they join a Waldorf school faculty. You can also find them in, *Towards a Deepening of Waldorf Education*, (published by the

Pedagogical Section of the School of Spiritual Science, Goetheanum, Dornach, Switzerland).

The retrospect, a "must" for teachers

There are meditations and concentration exercises that develop and strengthen our forces of thinking and conceptualizing. We enliven these forces by bringing will, movement, and creativity into our thinking. Life, movement, artistry, and creativity are not possible without guiding will into our thinking.

On the other hand, there are exercises that address the will. Since the will is a human capacity that functions below our threshold of consciousness, these exercises bring consciousness to the course of our destiny, to shine a light on it, so that we can gain at least some understanding and insight of our unfolding karma. In addition, we also try to shine a light into our daily interactions with others, to understand ourselves as social beings. With the will, our task is to bring what takes its course unconsciously into our consciousness.

Between these two there are exercises to unfold a heart culture, strongly community oriented. Here we can see the six essential exercises and the eightfold path exercises.

As mentioned previously, meditational practice is the only truly free deed that we can accomplish. This is also a reason why it is so difficult to stay with it! We begin with the best intentions, and then after a time of practicing, we start to make excuses why we cannot find the time on that day, and gradually we let go of our practice again. In this way we may spend years on-again, off-again, before we have developed the inner strength to stay with it.

The practice of the *rueckschau* or retrospect is a "must" for the teacher. On the one hand, teachers need to look back over the lessons, the day, and the interactions with the students. On the other hand, we teachers also need to look back on the various teachers meetings in a meditative way. This helps us to get to know our colleagues better, and to get to know ourselves. By looking back and calmly bringing the various situations before us, we learn to notice in a different way than the usual. That is when things are brought into consciousness. Permit me to bring a personal example. When I taught in Germany, I had forty-five children in my first grade. It was at night, when I looked back over my lessons of that day, that it came to my consciousness that I was able to recall clearly only about thirty-six children of my forty-five. I noticed that the ones I did not have livingly before me were the sweet little girls. I could not really remember how they participated on that day. This was also due to the fact that they did everything the teacher asked immediately. I could not picture how they had reacted to what I taught on that day, whether they were joyful and eager, or not so engaged.

I was deeply grateful for this exercise because having brought this to my consciousness at night, I could spend more time with the girls the following morning and make up for my lack of the previous day. This is an enormous benefit of this exercise: What otherwise would have slipped by me and remained in the sub- or semi-conscious sphere became clear and therefore open to change. I always felt that through this exercise especially, I could adjust my own karma (in a small way) because I could correct what I had omitted and improve where I had failed. In this way we can begin to take a small step toward rectifying mistakes and omissions in our present life. We do not wait for kamaloka, as the retrospect of life is called that we experience after death, to face the consequences of our deeds.

Looking back over the day

When we work with the retrospect, when we look backwards over our day in the evening, we bring before our mind's eye our daily (inter-) actions. We illumine them. We hear again what someone said to us, and we hear also how we responded. By recalling various situations in backwards order, we get to know ourselves, how we react, how we respond, and where our sensitivities are.

Looking at our life

We illumine the path through life by working in a similar manner, by bringing a certain age before us and situations that we remember. We linger with them. We take other situations. We will receive quite a good picture of how we were at these ages. It is a particular help for the teacher, to go back to the age of the students that she teaches, to recall what was important for her at that age, what she treasured, how she felt and so on. This retrospect exercise enriches the teacher's ability to identify with her students.

Reviewing the lessons

It should be a daily practice for the Waldorf teacher to recall what happened in her lessons. It is necessary to become conscious of how each activity went. How were the students engaged? Were they interested, bored, sleepy? Did they find other things to amuse them? If yes, why? Was I not able to bring enough pictures that engaged them? Was I myself interested in the subject I brought? (One should hope so!) What did I bring that was new today? Did it go well? What do I need to change? These and many more questions should be asked daily. We should end our daily session as teacher by asking ourselves: "What could I have done better?" This question needs to be answered in the next day's lesson.

I would like to end this book by saying:

Dear Colleagues,

I wanted to bring some of those things that must live in the souls of the teachers if the inherent promise of Waldorf education is to emerge further. If we succeed in this, then its healing power will continue to stream into our work and our schools. Strength and health are forces that originate in moral spiritual worlds. If we recognize and appreciate the uniqueness of Waldorf education as an education for this Michael age, then Waldorf education will be well. It will depend on you, dear colleagues, if and how the life stream will continue. Your commitment, your effort, is our future and the future of our children. Above and beyond all this, realize that as Waldorf teachers we are never alone. The beings of the third hierarchy are always with us. They wish to work with us whenever we make the effort to unite with them.

Notes

1 Steiner, *Spiritual Ground of Education*, Aug. 24, 1922.
2 Theodor Zdrazil, dissertation, 549.
3 Steiner, *Renewal of Education*, 109-110.
4 Steiner, *Renewal of Education*, 109-110.
5 Steiner, *Roots of Education*, 12-13.
6 Steiner, *Roots of Education*, 13.
7 Steiner, *Roots of Education*, 13.
8 Steiner, *Theosophy*, Chapter II.
9 Steiner, *Education of the Child*, 4.
10 Steiner, *Renewal of Education*, 29.
11 Steiner, *Study of Man*, 156.
12 Steiner, *Education of the Child*, 5-9.
13 Steiner, *Fundamentals of Therapy*, 11.
14 Gloeckler, *Journal Towards Health*, Lecture 1, Oct 2, 2009.
15 Steiner, *Education of the Child*, 9.
16 **Salutogenesis** is a term coined by Aaron Antonovsky, a professor of medical sociology. The term describes an approach focusing on factors that support human health and well-being, rather than on factors that cause disease.
17 Gloeckler, *Salutogenese*, 9.
18 Gloeckler, *Salutogenese*.
19 Steiner, *Practical Advice to Teachers*, Lecture 3, 40.
20 Steiner, *Roots of Education*, 42.
21 Steiner, *Education of the Child*, 10.
22 Steiner, *Knowledge of Higher Worlds*, 116.
23 Steiner, *Roots of Education,* 47.
24 Steiner, *Essentials of Education*, 8.
25 Gloeckler, *Zur Doppelnatur der Wesensglieder (The Double-Nature of the Human Subtle Bodies)*, 4.
26 Steiner, *Soul Economy*, 135-136.
27 Steiner, *Soul Economy*, 136.
28 Steiner, *Soul Economy*, 136-137.
29 Steiner, *Balance in Teaching*, 43-45.
30 Steiner, *Soul Economy*, 152.
31 Steiner, *Soul Economy*, 110-112.
32 Steiner, *Soul Economy*, 150-151.
33 Steiner, *Theosophy*, 65.
34 Steiner, *Theosophy*, 68.

35 Steiner, *Theosophy*, 113.
36 Steiner, *Theosophy*, 70.
37 Steiner, *Human Values in Education*, 133-134.
38 Steiner, *Soul Economy*, 133.
39 Steiner, *Roots of Education,* 36.
40 Steiner, *Roots of Education,* 36.
41 Steiner, *Education and Modern Spiritual Life*, 182-183.
42 Steiner, *Education and Modern Spiritual Life*, 183.
43 Steiner, *Education and Modern Spiritual Life*, 183.
44 Steiner, *Education and Modern Spiritual Life*, 185.
45 Steiner, *Education of the Child*, 31.
46 Steiner, *The Child's Changing Consciousness*, 29.
47 Spitzer, *Geist und Gehirn (Spirit and Brain).*
48 Steiner, *Soul Economy*, 137.
49 Hesse, *Kindheit des Zauberers*, (translation by author).
50 Walter, *Thema und Variationen*, (translation by author).
51 Jaspers, *Schicksal und Wille*, (translation by author).
52 Steiner, *Soul Economy,* 137-139.
53 Steiner, *Soul Economy*, 139.
54 Steiner, *Soul Economy*, 139-140.
55 Steiner, *Spiritual Ground of Education*, 41.
56 Steiner, *Spiritual Ground of Education*, 48.
57 Spitzer, *"Medizin fuer die Schule* (Medicine for Schools)," in *Lernen und Gehirn*, 28-29.
58 Spitzer, *"Medizin fuer die Schule* (Medicine for Schools)," in *Lernen und Gehirn*, 28-29.
59 Steiner, *Study of Man*, Lecture 4, 57.
60 Goleman, *Emotional Intelligence*, 36.
61 Steiner, *Study of Man*, Lecture 1, 19-20.
62 Steiner, *Practical Advice to Teachers*, 9.
63 Steiner, *Study of Man,* Lecture 1, 20.
64 Steiner, Overcoming Nervousness, 11-12.
65 Smit, *Der Werdende Mensch (The Expectant Human)*, 8.
66 Smit, *Der Werdende Mensch*, 39.
67 Steiner, *Essentials of Education*, 21.
68 Steiner, *Soul Economy*, 138.
69 Steiner, *Driving Force*, Lecture 1, 10.
70 Steiner, *Balance in Teaching*, Lecture 4.
71 Steiner, "The Work of the Angels in Man's Astral Body"
72 Golenhofen, *Physiology Today*, in Erziehungskunst #5, May 2003, 552.

73 Bauer, *Lob der Schule (Praise of Schools)*, 15-16.
74 Bauer, *Lob der Schule (Praise of Schools)*, 16.
75 Bauer, *Lob der Schule (Praise of Schools)*, 20.
76 Bauer, *Lob der Schule (Praise of Schools)*, 20, 23.
77 Hildebrandt, *Chronobiology and Chronomedicine*.
78 Spitzer, "*Medizin fuer die Schule* (Medicine for Schools)," in *Lernen und Gehirn*, 28-29.
79 Schoeffler, *Kind im Wandel des Jahrhunderts (Child in the Changing Century)*.
80 Steiner, *Erziehung und Leben*, Lecture 1, April 4, 1924, 169.
81 Steiner, *Education as a Force for Social Change*, 12.
82 Steiner, *Overcoming Nervousness*, 9, 11-12.
83 Steiner, *Renewal of Education*, 86.
84 Steiner, *Education of the Child*, 19-20.
85 I have translated this story from the German. Its author is unknown to me.
86 Steiner, *Essentials of Education*, 8.
87 Bandura, *Lernen am Modell (Learning from the Model)*.
88 Bauer, in Buccino et al, *European Journal of Neuroscience*.
89 Steiner, *Human Values*, Lecture 3, 23.
90 Steiner, *Human Values*, 29.
91 Steiner, *Spiritual Ground of Education*, 111-112.
92 Mueller, *Healing Forces in the Word and Its Rhythms*, 12.
93 Mueller, *Healing Forces in the Word and Its Rhythms*, 12.
94 Mueller, *Healing Forces in the Word and Its Rhythms*, 14.
95 Steiner, *Study of Man*, Lecture 4, 69.
96 Mueller, *Healing Forces in the Word and Its Rhythms*, 13.
97 Steiner, *Practical Advice to Teachers*, Lecture 3.
98 Steiner, *Practical Advice to Teachers*, 61.
99 Steiner, *Driving Force*, 10-11.
100 Steiner, *Renewal of Education*, 138-139.
101 Steiner, *Study of Man*, 128.
102 Steiner, *Study of Man*, 131.
103 Steiner, *Study of Man*, 131-132.
104 Steiner, *Curative Education*, Lecture 2, 39.
105 Steiner, *Essentials of Education*, 28.
106 Steiner, *Curative Education*, Lecture 2, 39.
107 Steiner, *Foundations of Human Experience*, 29.
108 Steiner, *Foundations of Human Experience*, 29.
109 Steiner, *Study of Man*, Lecture 1.
110 Pewtherer, ed., *Toward the Deepening of Waldorf Education*.

111 Steiner, *Mystery of the Trinity*, 76-77.
112 Steiner, *Mystery of the Trinity*, 77-78.

Bibliography

Avison, Kevin and Martin Rawson. *The Tasks and Content of the Steiner-Waldorf Curriculum.* Edinburgh, U.K.: Floris Books, 2014.

Bandura, Albert. *Lernen am Modell (Learning from the Model).* Stuttgart: Klett-Cotta, 1976.

Bauer, Joachim. *Lob der Schule (Praise of Schools).* Hamburg: Hoffmann und Campe, 2007.

Buccino, Giovanni et all. *fMRI Study.* Italy: University di Parma, 2001. European Journal of Neuroscience, Vol. 13.

Gloeckler, Michaela. *Mission of the Physician Teacher and Priest.* Journal Towards Health. Vancouver, Canada, Oct. 2, 2009.

___ . *Salutogenese.* Aktuelle Themen, Heft 5, Bad Liebenzell: Verein fuer Anthroposophisches Heilwesen, 2001.

___ et all. *Education–Health for Life.* Dornach: Medical and Pedagogical Section, 2006.

___. *Zur Doppelnatur der Wesensglieder ("The Double-Nature of the Human Subtle Members").* Goetheanum Lecture. Dornach, Switzerland, 2005.

Goleman, Daniel. *Emotional Intelligence.* New York: Bantam Books, 1995.

Golenhofen, K. *Physiology Today.* Munich, 2000, in: Erziehungskunst #5, May 2003.

Hesse, Hermann. *Kindheit des Zauberers (Childhood of the Magician).* Gesammelte Schriften, Bd 4, Frankfurt: Suhrkamp AG, 1957.

Hildebrandt, et all. *Chronobiology and Chronomedicine, "Biological Rhythms and Medical Consequences"* (in German). Stuttgart: Hippokrates, 1998.

Hurrelmann, K. *"Most Children Today are Young Adults,"* NZZ, Zuericher Zeitung, 25/26 Jan., 1997.

Jaspers, Karl. *Schicksal und Wille in Mitte der Kindheit.* Stuttgart: Freies Geistesleben, 1973.

Mueller, Heinz. *Healing Forces in the Word and Its Rhythms.* Fellowship Publications, Forest Row, U.K., 1983.

Smit, Jorgen. *Der Werdende Mensch.* Stuttgart: Verlag Freies Geistesleben, 1990.

Schoeffler, Herbert. *Kind im Wandel des Jahrhunderts (Child in the Changing Century).* Quoted in Medizinisch-Paedagogische Konferenz, Stuttgart, Heft 26, August 2003.

Spitzer, Manfred. *Medizin fuer die Schule (Medicine for Schools)* in: *Lernen und Gehirn (Learning and the Brain).* Ralf Caspary, editor. Freiburg: Verlag Herder, 2006.

Spitzer, Manfred. *Geist und Gehirn (Spirit and Brain).* Forschung und Wissen, Nr. 2, 2005.

Steiner, Rudolf. *Anthroposophic Spiritual Science and Medical Therapy.* N.Y.: Mercury Press, 1991, CW 213.

_ _ _. *Anweisungen fur eine Esoterische Schulung (Instructions for an Esoteric Schooling).* German edition, GA 42, 81.

_ _ _. *Balance in Teaching.* Gt. Barrington, MA: Anthroposophic Press, 2007, CW 302a.

_ _ _ . *The Child's Changing Consciousness.* Hudson, N.Y.: Anthroposophic Press, 1988, CW 306.

_ _ _ . *Curative Education.* London: Rudolf Steiner Press, 1972, CW 317.

_ _ _ . *The Driving Force of Spiritual Powers in World Evolution.* Toronto, Canada: Steiner Books Center, 1972, CW 222.

_ _ _ . *Education and Modern Spiritual Life.* London: Anthroposophic Publishing, 1954, CW 307.

_ _ _ . *Education as a Force for Social Change.* Hudson,N.Y.: Anthroposophic Press, CW 296.

_ _ _ . *The Education of the Child.* New York: Anthroposophic Press, 1996, CW 34.

_ _ _ . *Erziehung und Leben (Education and Life).* Dornach, 1998, CW 297a.

_ _ _ . *The Essentials of Education.* Great Barrington, MA: Anthroposophic Press, 1997, CW 308.

_ _ _ . *The Foundation of Human Experience.* Hudson, N.Y.: Anthroposophic Press, 1996, CW 293.

_ _ _ . *Fundamentals of Therapy.* Chestnut Ridge, N.Y.: Mercury Press, 1999, CW 27.

___. *Human Values in Education*. London: Rudolf Steiner Press, 1971, CW 310.

___. *Knowledge of Higher Worlds*. Gt. Barrington, MA: Anthroposophic Press, 2002, CW 10.

___. *The Mystery of the Trinity*. Hudson, N.Y.: Anthroposophic Press, 1991, CW 214.

___. *Overcoming Nervousness*. New York: Anthroposophic Press, 1969, CW 143.

___. *Practical Advice to Teachers*. London: Rudolf Steiner Press, 1961, CW 294.

___. *The Renewal of Education*. Forest Row, U.K.: Fellowship Publications, 1981, CW 301.

___. *The Roots of Education*. New York: Anthroposophic Press, 1997, CW 309.

___. *Soul Economy*. Gt. Barrington, MA: Anthroposophic Press, 2003, CW 303.

___. *The Spiritual Ground of Education*. London: Anthroposophic Publishing House, 1947, CW 305.

___. *Study of Man*. Forest Row, U.K.: Rudolf Steiner Press, 2007, CW 293.

___. *Theosophy*. New York: Anthroposophic Press, 1994, CW 9.

___. *Towards the Deepening of Waldorf Education: Excerpts from the Work of Rudolf Steiner*. Essays and Documents. Edited James Pewtherer. Dornach: Philosophisch-Anthroposophischer Verlag am Goetheanum, 2012.

___. *The Work of the Angels in Man's Astral Body*. New York: Rudolf Steiner Press, 1960, CW 182.

Stockmeyer, E.A. Karl. *Rudolf Steiner's Curriculum for Waldorf Schools*. Edinburgh, U.K.: Steiner Schools Fellowship Publications, May, 2015.

Walter, Bruno. *Thema und Variationen (Theme and Variation)*. Frankfurt am Main, Fischer Verlag, 1960.

Zdrazil, Theodor. *Dissertation*, Stuttgart: Erziehungskunst #5, May, 2003.